Women's Human Rights

CHARLOTTE BUNCH AND NIAMH REILLY

published by:

Center for Women's Global Leadership,
Rutgers University, New Jersey, USA

 United Nations Development Fu
for Women (UNIFEM)
New York, USA

The views expressed in this book are those of the authors and do not necessarily represent the views of UNIFEM, the United Nations or any of its affiliated organizations.

Demanding Accountability: The Global Campaign and Vienna Tribunal for Women's Human Rights
C. Bunch, N. Reilly
ISBN 0-912917-29-6

The Center for Women's Global Leadership
Douglass College, Rutgers University, 27 Clifton Avenue, New Brunswick, NJ 08903 USA
Phone: (908) 932-8782 Fax: (908) 932-1180

United Nations Development Fund for Women
304 East 45th Street, 6th floor, New York, NY 10017 USA
Phone: (212) 906-6400 Fax (212) 906-6705

All UNIFEM publications are distributed by Women, Ink.
777 UN Plaza, 3rd Floor, New York, NY 10017 USA
Phone: (212) 687-8633 Fax (212) 661-2704

Cover & book design by Emerson, Wajdowicz Studios, Inc
1123 Broadway, New York, NY 10010 USA

Desktop Operator: Cynthia Madansky

Photo Credits: Cindy Ewing

Table of Contents

Acknowledgements

To name all who have contributed to the Global Campaign for Women's Human Rights, the Global Tribunal on Violations of Women's Human Rights and this book is impossible. Nevertheless, at the risk of leaving some out, we want to mention a few who have been particularly important to us. Above all, we must emphasize that the movement behind this book is the product of the collective wisdom, vision, and work of many women throughout the world.

The Center for Women's Global Leadership could never have launched this campaign without the cooperation of many groups internationally, but we wish to thank especially those organizations whose ongoing collaboration in developing the campaign was crucial: Asian Women's Human Rights Council, Austrian Women's Human Rights Working Group, Feminist International Radio Endeavor (FIRE), Human Rights Watch Women's Project, International Women's Tribune Centre, ISIS International, United Nations Development Fund for Women (UNIFEM), Women in Law and Development in Africa (WiLDAF), and Women Living Under Muslim Laws International Solidarity Network. Locally our work was enhanced enormously by the New York/New Jersey area Working Group on Women's Human Rights, and we appreciate all those who attended its meetings and helped to develop strategies with us there.

The Campaign has benefitted from the leadership and guidance of many, but we have especially depended upon a core of strong feminists from around the world including but not limited to: Sunila Abeyesekera, Gladys Acosta, Georgina Ashworth, Ariane Brunet, Florence Butegwa, Roxanna Carrillo, Rebecca Cook, Rhonda Copelon, Alda Facio, Hina Jilani, Leni Marin, Rosa Logar, Suzanne Roach, Lourdes Sajor, María Suárez, Dorothy Thomas, and Anne Walker.

For The Global Tribunal, we must express our deep gratitude to the women who testified, the judges, the moderators and the opening speakers—all of whom are listed in the programme (Document C in Part IV) and most of whom are quoted in Part II. In addition, we thank the International Coordinating Committee, the legal counselors, the Communications Consortium, Gerry Rogers of Augusta Productions, Helene Rosenbluth, Ingeborg Schwarz, Valerie Oosterveld, and all those from many countries who helped to prepare testimony and who supported those who testified.

The staff, interns, and associates of the Global Center over the past few years maintained the daily work of the campaign and prepared for the Tribunal. In particular, Raahi Reddi, Andrea Romaní, Sita Venkateswar, and Tamara Xavier of our Center along with Meera Singh from IWTC and Jennifer Klot from UNIFEM were support staff for The Tribunal in Vienna. Global Center staff members Diana Gerace and Susana Fried kept the work going back home. Other affiliates of the Center who helped with aspects of the campaign include: Asma Abdel Halim, Rosa Briceño, Seble Dawit, Sam Frost, Cici Kinsman, Lori Heise, Stephanie Lentini, Linda Posluszny, and Susan Roche.

In the preparation of this book, we express great appreciation for the assistance of Sam Frost—she has edited, proofread, and backed up all that is here and for Joanne Sandler who has made the co-publishing with UNIFEM a pleasure. For personal support and constant intellectual challenge in seeking to complete this book, we thank Roxanna Carrillo, Susana Fried, and Ed Hatton.

The Center could not have done any of this work without the steady backing of Mary Hartman, the Dean of Douglass College which houses us, the Associate Alumnae of Douglass College, and the support of many within the Rutgers University community. Finally, we want to thank those who have expressed their confidence in this work as funders (listed at the end of this book), and especially Margaret Schink, June Zeitlin, and Carmen Barroso for their strong commitment to women's human rights and their trust in us to carry out this work.

Preface

hroughout history, women have been absent from those arenas in which important decisions concerning the political definition of rights have taken place. Women have been confined to a space of shadows and domesticity, a situation which was well-expressed by Xenophon in the fourth century BC: "The Gods have created women for the domestic functions and men for all other functions." The fight for the recognition of women's humanity, and thus of their entitlement to human rights, has a long history that continues to the present day. To be confined to only one social space, the home, has meant that through the centuries men have played the role of intermediary between women and all the other spheres of social life. To mediate such a relationship is a formidable exercise of power, even for those men who do not have access to wealth and social prestige.

If there is one intriguing pattern that seems to cut across centuries and different civilizations, it is that a woman is always less entitled to rights than a man. This is so in spite of the inequalities of social class, race, ethnicity, religion, and culture that permeate societies and affect both men and women. Perhaps it is this puzzling universality that helps to explain why, more and more, women's movements for equity and social dignity are becoming international.

I consider the Global Campaign for Women's Human Rights and its Global Tribunal on Violations of Women's Human Rights to be a central and key part of this process. The international campaign which called upon the United Nations to recognize that violence against women is a human rights violation reflects a growing movement that is grounded in the assumption that Women's Rights are Human Rights.

The Tribunal was a successful and most necessary event that clearly revealed to governments, UN officials, and other sectors of the NGO world the extent to which women are submitted to violence, the wide-spread incidence of so-called domestic violence, and the general disrespect that exists for women's physical and emotional integrity. The Tribunal testimonies, by women from very different countries and backgrounds, are pieces of a unique tapestry that point to a common story of disrespect and violation that occurs even today at the turn of the century. Since neither nationality, class, race nor religion are determining factors in either the roots or prevalence of such violence, The Tribunal called for a revision of the concepts of public and private spheres, and of individual and social rights, in the formulation of national and international laws and regulations.

The Tribunal is also evidence of a failure, the failure of most societies to recognize women as full citizens, as human beings who are entitled to civic, social and political rights, to the recognition of themselves as human beings, and thus to protection by national and international human laws and procedures.

Using different strategies and instruments, women continue to build roads that will lead them, as full citizens, into the national and international public arenas. Let us keep working together for a time when campaigns and tribunals like this will no longer be necessary.

Jacqueline Pitanguy
Rio de Janeiro, Brazil
Director of CEPIA (Citizenship Studies, Information, Action)

Part I
The Road to Vienna

Chapter 1
The Global Campaign for Women's Human Rights

The United Nations *Universal Declaration of Human Rights*, proclaimed in 1948, states unconditionally that it applies to all human beings "without distinction of any kind such as race, colour, sex, language...or other status" (Article 2). Nevertheless, many violations of women's human rights continue to be ignored, condoned, and perpetrated by societies and governments in every region of the world. A particularly clear example is gender-based violence against women, which has not been understood as a human rights issue much less as one requiring attention from the international human rights community.

It came as no surprise, therefore, that the United Nations resolution to hold its second World Conference on Human Rights (the first had taken place in 1968) did not mention women or recognize any gender-specific aspects of human rights in its proposed agenda. Yet, by the time the World Conference ended in Vienna in June 1993, gender-based violence and women's human rights emerged as one of the most talked-about subjects, and women were recognized as a well-organized human rights constituency. The final statement issued by the 171 participating governments at the Conference—The Vienna Declaration—devotes several pages to treating the "equal status and human rights of women" as a priority for governments and the United Nations; further, it sounds an historic call to recognize the elimination of "violence against women in public and private life" as a human rights obligation. This progress on women's human rights did not happen by accident.

Over the past four decades, the international human rights community has focused primarily on certain aspects of civil and political human rights, which address important but limited concerns such as the denial of freedom of expression, arbitrary arrest, torture in detention, and the death penalty when perpetrated by state actors. Some non-governmental organizations (NGOs) have lobbied with moderate success to broaden the implementation of human rights through specific conventions, working groups, and/or special rapporteurs in areas such as the right to development and rights of the child, as well as on topics like disappearances, racial discrimination, religious intolerance, and contemporary forms of slavery. However, the United Nations' *International Covenant on Civil and Political Rights* (ICCPR) still receives more resources than other human rights instruments and has more effective implementation mechanisms; it therefore plays a predominant role in the practice of human rights globally. This approach to human rights, which gives priority to protecting citizens from certain types of direct state coercion, also facilitates the "protection" of male-defined cultural, family or religious rights often at the expense of human rights of women. Further, the failure to develop effective measures to monitor violations and secure implementation of socio-economic rights has hindered the recognition of systemic gender-based socio-economic violations which prevail in every region.

The Global Campaign for Women's Human Rights—a loose coalition of groups and individuals worldwide working for women's human rights—seeks to demonstrate both how traditionally accepted human rights abuses are specifically affected by gender, and how many other violations against women have remained invisible within prevailing approaches to human rights. For example, violations of women's human rights committed in the "private sphere" of the home, or in the context of familial or intimate relationships, have not been considered within the purview of a government's human rights obligations.

The challenge from women in Vienna, and the increased awareness of the human rights of women there, reflected the movement around women's human rights that has emerged over the past decade. This process has its roots in the growth of diverse women's movements globally during the United Nations Decade for Women (1976-85). Since then, women have continually raised the question of why "women's rights" and women's lives have been deemed secondary to the "human rights" and lives of men. Declaring that "women's rights **are** human rights," women sought to make clear that widespread gender-based discrimination and abuse of women is a devastating reality as urgently in need of redress as other human rights violations. More women die each day from various forms of gender-based discrimination and violence than from any other type of human rights abuse. This ranges from female infanticide and the disproportionate malnutrition of girl children, to the multiple forms of coercion, battery, mutilation, sexual assault and murder that large numbers of women face in every region of the world, throughout their lives, simply because they are female.

Organizing for Change

While a variety of women have raised these questions for some time, a coordinated effort to change this attitude using a human rights framework gained momentum in the early 1990's. Various international, regional and local women's groups began meeting to strategize on how to make women's human rights perspectives more visible. In 1991, the Center for Women's Global Leadership (Global Center) convened a New York area working group on women's human rights. This group was composed of women from many countries who were living in the area and working in human rights and women's NGOs, as well as at UN agencies and area universities. This working group has continued to meet to discuss conceptual issues and plan strategies for women's human rights, and has parallels in other cities around the world.

The UN World Conference on Human Rights became a natural vehicle to highlight the transformative visions of human rights thinking and practice being developed by such groups. The Center's active focus on the World Conference began at its 1991 Women's Global Leadership Institute, where participants developed the idea of an annual campaign of *16 Days of Activism Against Gender Violence*, linking the International Day Against Violence Against Women (November 25), to International Human Rights Day (December 10).[1] The *16 Days* campaign has grown steadily since then, involving women's groups in dozens of

---

[1] November 25 was declared International Day Against Violence Against Women by the first Feminist Encuentro for Latin America and the Caribbean in 1981, Bogota, Colombia. The day commemorates the Mirabal sisters who were brutally murdered by the Trujillo dictatorship in the Dominican Republic in 1960. December 10 celebrates the anniversary of the Universal Declaration of Human Rights proclaimed in 1948. The period also includes World AIDS Day (December 1), and the anniversary of the Montreal massacre (December 6) when a man gunned down 14 engineering students for being "feminists."

countries who have organized hundreds of events, including petition drives, hearings, demonstrations, lobbying, media campaigns, street theatre, cultural festivals, radio programs, panels, and the production of buttons, t-shirts and posters.

During the first *16 Days* campaign in 1991, a petition drive was initiated which called upon the United Nations World Conference on Human Rights "to comprehensively address women's human rights at every level of its proceedings" and to recognize "gender violence, a universal phenomenon which takes many forms across culture, race, and class... as a violation of human rights requiring immediate action." The petition, originally sponsored by the Center for Women's Global Leadership and the International Women's Tribune Centre (IWTC), was distributed in English, Spanish, and French through dozens of women's networks. It was subsequently translated into 23 languages and used by women in many different ways at the local, national, and regional levels. By the time of the World Conference, over 1000 sponsoring groups had gathered almost a half million signatures from 124 countries.

At the same time, regional movements for women's human rights were working to transform the limited interpretations and applications of human rights in their areas. At the regional preparatory meetings for the Vienna World Conference held in Tunis, San Jose, and Bangkok, women demanded that the human rights of women be discussed. For example, groups in Latin America organized a women's human rights conference called *La Nuestra (Ours)* prior to the regional meeting in San José. They prepared a *19 Point Agenda* to be presented there which women from other regions also utilized.[2] Women were also an active presence at various national preparatory meetings, and held other non-governmental events aimed at influencing the World Conference agenda. For example, Women in Law and Development in Africa (WiLDAF) organized a series of sub-regional meetings where participants defined their own human rights concerns and then drew up a regional women's paper which was presented at the final international Preparatory Committee meeting in Geneva in April, 1993.[3] Since the Asian regional meeting was held very late in the preparatory process, Asian women were able to use work that had already been done in other regions and globally. Despite frequent oppo-

---

[2] For a detailed description see *Satellite Meeting "La Nuestra."* Feminist International Radio Endeavor, Costa Rica. 1992.

[3] See *The World Conference on Human Rights: The WiLDAF Experience.* ed. Butegwa, F. Women in Law and Development in Africa, 1993.

sition from their governments, they drew upon these efforts as well as their own regionally specific initiatives to integrate women's issues and perspectives into the final Asian NGO statement.

Regional, national and global documents were written, exchanged and revised by women in this process, and several international gatherings were held to develop some common points of emphasis to present in Vienna. In February 1993, the Center for Women's Global Leadership organized a Strategic Planning Institute[4] to focus on how women could most effectively influence events at the Vienna conference. The meeting brought together a small group of women from around the world who had already made significant strides toward addressing women's rights as human rights regionally and locally. The specific tasks of the meeting were twofold: 1) working on lobbying strategies for the UN World Conference, which included further development of a set of recommendations on women's human rights to be used at the final preparatory meeting and in Vienna itself; and 2) planning women's non-governmental activities at Vienna and, in particular, a global tribunal on women's human rights.[5]

In addition to those groups already mentioned, other regional networks, such as the Asian Women's Human Rights Council and CLADEM (Latin American Committee for Women's Rights), and international organizations like Change Inc. and the International Human Rights Law Group were also mobilizing to put women's concerns on the governmental agenda for Vienna. (See *Part IV, Documents B* and *H* for reports on other organizing efforts around the Vienna Conference.) By the time of the final meeting of the international Preparatory Committee held in Geneva in April 1993, which was to draft the Conference document for Vienna, women were prepared with common demands to present to the governments.

Meanwhile, there was still uncertainty about whether the Conference would even be held. In two prior international Preparatory Committee meetings, the governments had not been able to agree on the conference agenda nor to start

---

[4] The results of this meeting are included in *International Campaign for Women's Human Rights 1992-93 Report.* Center for Women's Global Leadership, 1993.

[5] Most UN World Conferences, which are meetings attended by government delegations, are accompanied by parallel NGO activities which generally include panels, workshops, public events, and lobbying activities. These parallel activities may precede or coincide with the governmental meetings . Increasingly, the NGOs who participate in the parallel activities work together to produce a coherent NGO statement addressing the official conference agenda. In Vienna, the NGO Forum was organized jointly by the NGO Planning Committee in Geneva and the Vienna-based Boltzmann Institute for Human Rights, and was held on June 10-12 immediately preceding the UN World Conference.

drafting the document for it. These meetings had split, primarily along North-South lines, over the questions of which human rights issues had priority (socio-economic versus civil and political) and what rights should be considered universal. Thus, at the opening of the final Geneva Preparatory Committee meeting there was still no agreed-upon text to serve as a basis for the agenda for the UN World Conference. This provided an important opportunity for women who had focused on building coalitions across North-South lines and addressing socio-economic as well as civil and political rights, to get their ideas included in the Conference agenda.

The women's caucus at the final meeting of the International Preparatory Committee included representatives of international women's and human rights non-governmental organizations that are often present at such gatherings, as well as Third World women active in their regional processes, many of whom were organized to attend through the United Nations Development Fund for Women (UNIFEM). This coalition crossed longtime divisions, not only along North-South lines, but also between women working in government, in non-governmental organizations, and in United Nations agencies. The women's caucus succeeded in two critical areas: first, it effectively pressured for the inclusion of text on women in the draft document which was accepted by governments at the Geneva meeting almost without reservation—a process which virtually assured its passage later in Vienna; and second, it formed the basis for many women to continue working together across these lines in Vienna. (The lobbying process for the final *Vienna Declaration* is discussed further in Chapter Ten of this book.)

This phase of active lobbying for the inclusion of women in the Vienna proceedings, and in the international human rights agenda generally, was accompanied by grassroots hearings which were launched as part of the second *16 Days of Activism* campaign in 1992. The Global Center and IWTC sent out a call with suggestions for how to hold such hearings, and also distributed a revised UN documentation form for receiving complaints that took more account of women. The hearings aimed at giving voice to gender-based human rights violations, articulating more precisely the spectrum of issues behind the global petition drive for recognition of women's human rights.

From November 1992 on, women held hearings to document individual complaints and group cases of violations of women's human rights. Public hearings were convened in diverse places such as Argentina, Costa Rica, India, Nepal, and the United States, and dozens of speakouts were held in other locations to document female human rights abuse. (See *Part IV, Document B* for a fuller account of these events.) The resulting testimonials were recorded, and the documentation sent to the UN Centre for Human Rights, providing concrete evidence of the need for human rights mechanisms that are more responsive to women's lives. Many women who could not hold hearings also gathered available information and documented female human rights abuses. These records informed submissions to the final international Preparatory Committee meeting and to the Conference itself.

Throughout the spring, women from diverse regions exchanged perspectives and information regarding these hearings and other women's workshops and initiatives that were being organized as part of the NGO activities in Vienna. Two of the major strategies that emerged from this process and which ensured women's visibility at the Vienna meeting were *The Rights Place for Women* (See *Chapter Nine* for a detailed description) and *The Global Tribunal on Violations of Women's Human Rights.*

The Global Tribunal on Violations of Women's Human Rights, which took place on June 15, 1993 in Vienna, gave vivid expression to the life and death consequences of women's human rights violations. It provided graphic demonstration of how being female can be life threatening, subjecting some women to torture, terrorism and slavery daily. The Global Tribunal called international attention to a pattern of female human rights abuse which must be taken seriously if human rights are to be an effective and credible component of the global political and economic order for the 21st century. This book focuses on The Global Tribunal and the movement for women's human rights from which it originated.

Chapter 2
Concept and Organization of The Global Tribunal

Purpose of the Tribunal

The idea of convening a Global Tribunal on Violations of Women's Human Rights at the 1993 World Conference on Human Rights emerged from a variety of discussions over several months amongst those active in the Global Campaign for Women's Human Rights in different regions. Previous events, such as the World Women's Congress for a Healthy Planet (Miami, 1991), the International Tribunal on Crimes against Women (Brussels, 1976), and various People's Tribunals, were mentioned as sources of inspiration by many who suggested that we undertake a Tribunal in the field of women's human rights.

The Tribunal was also a natural extension of the worldwide petition drive and hearings campaign launched as part of the *16 Days of Activism Against Gender Violence* in 1991 and 1992. Many of those who had become involved in the petition drive calling for the inclusion of women in the World Conference agenda were asking, what next? How do we show more clearly what it means for women's perspectives to be incorporated into human rights? With these concerns in mind, the Global Center and IWTC launched the Second Annual *16 Days of Activism* in 1992 with a call for international hearings and for increased documentation of violations of women's human rights which women wanted the World Conference and the international human rights community to address. The Tribunal was seen as an event that would draw upon these local and regional hearings and mark the culmination of several years of campaigning for the recognition of women's human rights.

The Tribunal was to be part of the non-governmental parallel activities taking place in Vienna during the UN World Conference and was to help inform human rights NGOs about women's human rights. In addition, the Tribunal intended to formally address the governmental delegates, and therefore was planned for the second day of the UN World Conference so that it would immediately call attention to the demand that the conference address gender-specific human rights concerns. The Tribunal was also understood as a way to utilize the media present at the World Conference, not only to reach the delegates in Vienna, but also to bring greater mainstream attention to female human rights abuses and violence against women generally.

The final decision to hold a tribunal, and the development of guidelines for it, took place at the Strategic Planning Institute convened by the Global Center in February 1993. Institute participants agreed that the over-arching objective should be to provide a global forum in which to demonstrate the failure of existing human rights mechanisms to promote and protect the human rights of women. (This placed it in the context of the UN World Conference agenda, which was to review and appraise the effectiveness of human rights machinery internationally.) The testimonies that women would recount at The Tribunal were to be symbolic of the situation of many thousands of women who could not be there. They would define, document, and make visible violations of women which the current conceptualization and practice of human rights had not adequately addressed. By bringing patterns of gender-based human rights violations to the foreground, Tribunal speakers would make women's challenges to the international human rights community concrete. This tactic was essential, for if human rights are to be a defining value for people into the 21st century they must be more universal; women, as well as all men, must have greater recourse to human rights instruments as a means of contesting abuses of their humanity.

The Tribunal planners sought to pose key challenges to the United Nations, national governments, and the international human rights community in several areas. In particular, it sought to:

▶ **Demonstrate obstacles to women's enjoyment of human rights that stem** from the distinction between public and private, especially around violence against women.

Human rights abuses committed against women and girls—from rape and battery, to forced sterilization, compulsory marriage and sexual exploitation—are acts of "cruel and inhuman treatment." For millions of women they constitute "torture" and the denial of "life, liberty and security of person." Yet, traditional human rights practice has relied upon a biased understanding of "public" and "private" spheres, whereby violations experienced by men as citizens tend to be more readily acknowledged as important than those experienced by women in the so-called private domain. The Tribunal was to challenge this distinction by demonstrating the impact on women's lives of gender-based violations in many contexts, whether perpetrated by state actors or by private individuals.

▶ **Expose the often ignored violations of female human rights in war and conflict situations.**

As the Tribunal was being planned in early 1993, international attention focused on the conflict in the former Yugoslavia and the use of rape and forced pregnancy as modes of ethnic cleansing. The UN World Conference offered an opportunity to expand people's understanding of this issue by showing how gender-based violence is used as a military strategy in many conflict situations. Thus, the case of the former Yugoslavia was to be presented in the context of other military abuses of women in contemporary and historical conflicts, such as Somalia, Peru, and Palestine as well as during World War II.

▶ **Reassert that women's human rights are indivisible and universal, and highlight the ways in which some claims to cultural and religious rights impede the universality of human rights with respect to women.**

The human rights of women must be unconditionally protected and cannot be negated in the interest of claims made by some regarding ethnicity, culture or religion. Religious fundamentalism—Christian, Hindu, Jewish, Islamic or any other—which seeks to enforce its edicts through prohibitions on women's freedom, either in terms of violations of bodily integrity, or the exclusion of women from social, political and economic power, cannot be tolerated if human rights are to be realized for all. Similarly, traditional practices which are intrinsically injurious to women and girls can find no justification or immunity in a human rights framework that claims to be universal.

‣ **Illustrate the gender-specific dimensions of already recognized international human rights violations.**

Women experience many of the same human rights violations as men, but there are often unrecognized aspects to this abuse that are based on gender. For example, attacks against non-combatants in conflict situations is a recognized violation of guaranteed human rights, but rape of women in these situations has only just begun to be recognized as such. Similarly, female prisoners and female relatives of detainees often experience sexual violation as a form of torture at the hands of state agents. Gender-based persecution must be exposed in relation to many other areas such as the conduct of so-called peace-keeping troops or refugee and humanitarian aid policies.

‣ **Underscore the implications for women of the secondary status of social, economic and cultural rights relative to political and civil rights.**

Human rights are called indivisible. Yet, as long as women are socially, economically, and culturally discriminated against and marginalized, the conditions for the realization of their human rights often do not exist. For example, the undervaluation of women's work and the exploitation of women in the global economy make women more vulnerable to further human rights abuses, such as family violence, compulsory marriage and forced prostitution.

‣ **Evaluate the effectiveness of human rights instruments, procedures, bodies and agencies, including non-governmental human rights organizations, in protecting and advocating for the human rights of women.**

Cases can be used to show how countries that have ratified various human rights treaties and conventions have failed to implement them in relation to women. There is also a need to expose government reservations to conventions that are gender-biased, and in the case of the United Nations Convention on the Elimination of All Forms of Discrimination Against Women, to challenge reservations that are counter to the intention of the convention. Governments must be urged to ratify conventions which might be effective in defending women's human rights.

‣ **Show that violations of women's human rights occur in both industrialized and "less developed" countries.**

The Tribunal organizers included a number of cases involving violations of women's human rights in the North in order to dispel the widespread attitude that human rights violations are confined to so-called underdeveloped countries. This was particularly important because, while there is no country in which women's human rights are secure, industrialized countries often champion women's causes abroad even as they ignore their plight at home.

Finally, The Tribunal, as part of the Global Campaign for Women's Human Rights, was envisioned as a process which would contribute to many other NGO activities throughout the two-week Conference in Vienna. All of these activities aimed at exploring the concrete responses which states, governments, and the international human rights community must make to end violations of women's human rights globally.

The Organizing Process

At the Global Center's February 1993 Strategic Planning Institute, an International Coordinating Committee (ICC) was formed to collaborate with the Global Center on the selection of Tribunal speakers and on related logistical work. The ICC eventually included: Asma Abdel Halim (WiLDAF, Sudan); Marion Bethel (CAFRA, Bahamas); Florence Butegwa (WiLDAF, Zimbabwe); Roxanna Carrillo (UNIFEM); Winde Evenhuis (HOM, Netherlands); Alda Facio (ILANUD, Costa Rica); Hina Jilani (AGHS Legal Aid, Pakistan); Nelia Sancho Liao (Asian Women's Human Rights Council, Philippines); Rosa Logar (Austrian Women's Shelter Network); Annette Pypops (Match International Centre, Canada); Ana Sisnett (Fund for a Compassionate Society, USA); María Suárez (FIRE, Costa Rica); and Anne Walker (IWTC). In addition the Asia and Pacific Forum on Women, Law and Development (APWLD), the Family Violence Prevention Fund in San Francisco, and the International Solidarity Network of Women Living Under Muslim Laws (WLUML) joined as organizational sponsors for the Tribunal.

The Tribunal format was structured so that the challenges outlined in the previous sections would be addressed through five inter-connected thematic sessions:

▶ Human Rights Abuse in the Family

▶ War Crimes Against Women

- Violations of Women's Bodily Integrity
- Socio-Economic Violations of Women's Human Rights
- Gender-based Political Persecution and Discrimination

In the selection of Tribunal themes and of cases to present, the ICC worked to ensure diversity of issues and regions, as well as of race, ethnicity, socio-economic class, sexual orientation and physical ability. Testimonies were made by both advocates for women who had been subject to human rights violations, and by women who wished to testify for themselves.

Following the Strategic Planning Institute, members of the ICC worked with women's organizations locally to identify cases for The Tribunal which best represented the concerns of their region. It was important that potential participants understood that The Tribunal could not produce a binding legal resolution for any of the cases presented. Rather, it would contribute to a broader political movement for the recognition of women's human rights so that cases like theirs would be handled better in the future. Members of the ICC identified four or five possible participants from each region. Working with the Center for Women's Global Leadership, ICC members ultimately selected 33 women from 25 countries to testify in accordance with The Tribunal's mandate.

Recognizing that participation in The Tribunal could be a stressful and emotional experience, ICC members sought to ensure that the testifiers from their regions would be accompanied to Vienna by a "support person" who would be available throughout the preparations for the Tribunal, at the event itself, and afterwards if needed. For the most part, the Global Center worked with IWTC and UNIFEM to raise the funds necessary to cover the costs of Tribunal participants, and in some instances those of the support person as well. (A complete list of donors to the Campaign and Tribunal is included at the end of the book.)

With the assistance of local women's groups and support persons, Tribunal speakers prepared ten-minute statements. When possible, the testifiers were asked to forward their written testimonies, short biographies, and a photograph (optional) in advance so that testimony could be coordinated better and information packets for the media prepared. On the Sunday prior to The Tribunal, all testifiers met for an orientation session with Tribunal organizers where they were also introduced to each other. They talked with the other women testifying in their segment and with the moderators for their sessions to review how the presentations would go. Several of the moderators also worked with women from their segments throughout the next day, further developing the testimony and building the morale of the testifiers. The moderators, who introduced the topics to be addressed in each session, were women from different regions who had been active in the Global Campaign. They were, in the order of the sessions: Monica O'Connor (Irish Women's Aid); Nelia Sancho Liao (Asian Women Human Rights Council); Gladys Acosta (Latin American Institute for Alternative Legal Services); Florence Butegwa (Women, Law and Development in Africa); and Charlotte Bunch (Center for Women's Global Leadership).

The auditorium in which The Tribunal took place seated 600 and was equipped with simultaneous translation, a large-screen, video and slide projectors and audio equipment. Where the testimony was not in a UN language, a support person acted as an interpreter during The Tribunal itself, and her interpretation into one of the UN languages was transmitted to the other interpreters. In addition, IWTC collaborated with the Global Center to coordinate the technical logistics so that several testifiers could incorporate video footage, slides, photographs and posters into their presentations.

The participants at the Strategic Planning Institute also developed criteria for the selection of a panel of 4-6 judges, to include both men and women, who would be supportive and in a position to effect change on the level of policy and/or public awareness. Judges were sought who would have some or all of the following traits: demonstrate a commitment to advancing the position of women; possess human rights expertise; be internationally recognizable; be influential with her/his peers and within the UN community; and have the stature to command media attention. ICC members agreed to consult with their broader networks and to nominate judges from their regions.

Once the nominations were compiled, the following distinguished judges agreed to preside over The Tribunal in Vienna: Gertrude Mongella, Secretary-General of the United Nations Fourth World Conference on Women and former Tanzanian High Commissioner to India; Justice P.N. Bhagwati, former Chief Justice of the Supreme Court of India and Chair of the Asian human rights NGO, AWARE; Ed Broadbent, a former Canadian Member of Parliament and President of the International Centre for Human Rights and Democratic Development in Montreal;

and Elizabeth Odio, Minister of Justice in Costa Rica and a member of the UN Committee Against Torture. Odio was later appointed as a judge on the War Crimes Commission for the conflict in the former Yugoslavia. Mary Robinson, President of Ireland, was invited to be the fifth judge, but she was unable to attend the Vienna Conference and sent a written statement of support to The Tribunal instead.

The judges sought to assess accountability for the human rights abuses presented by those testifying at The Tribunal, to delineate the human rights principles and agreements which had been violated, and to make concrete suggestions on how to redress violations of women's human rights. They worked in consultation with an advisory committee of women lawyers from different regions: Rebecca Cook (University of Toronto Law School, Canada); Alda Facio (ILANUD, Costa Rica); Ratna Kapur (Legal Advocate, India); and Mona Zulficar (Shalakany Law Office, Egypt). At the end of each of The Tribunal's thematic sessions, one of the judges responded specifically to the cases in that segment. The advisory committee worked with the judges both as they drafted their individual responses and as they wrote the final collective statement which was delivered at The Tribunal's closing session. (The judges' final statement is in Chapter Eight.)

Part II
The Tribunal:
Women Demand
Accountability

Gender-specific human rights abuses of women have been ignored, condoned, or committed by societies and governments in every region of the world for so long that they are often invisible even to human rights activists. Therefore, throughout its activities, the Global Campaign for Women's Human Rights has sought to make visible the ways in which women suffer gender-based human rights abuse. The Global Tribunal on Violations of Women's Human Rights at the UN World Conference on Human Rights was planned as a concrete demonstration—both to the Conference participants and to the world more generally—of how being female is a risk factor that makes many women vulnerable to routine forms of torture, terrorism, slavery, and abuse that have gone unchecked for too long.

*The 33 women who presented testimony to the Global Tribunal on Violations of Women's Human Rights at the Austria Centre in Vienna on June 15, 1993 conveyed the urgency of realizing the slogan: women's rights **are** human rights. In speaking out, these women shattered the wall of silence which has surrounded abuses of women's human rights, and squarely posed major challenges to governments and the international human rights community, demanding that violations of women's human rights be stopped. Some of the speakers delivered statements regarding the status of women's human rights in their regions or addressed general areas of women's abuse around the world. Others presented personal accounts of human rights violations they themselves had suffered, or spoke on behalf of women who were not present. Whether they stood up as critics or victims of an unjust system, all of the testifiers also spoke for the hundreds of thousands of women around the world who could not be in Vienna, and for whom the testimonies served to symbolize their lived experiences.*

Charlotte Bunch (Center for Women's Global Leadership), Johanna Dohnal (the Austrian Minister for Women's Affairs) and Marjorie Thorpe (the Deputy Director of UNIFEM) opened The Tribunal proceedings. Minister Dohnal exhorted the international human rights community to include the "specific experiences of women" in "traditional approaches to human rights in order to protect women's lives as well as the lives of men." She concluded her remarks by stating that "there is no need to...[wish women] success here today, because our all being here today fighting for women's rights is already a success."

Marjorie Thorpe anticipated that "the testimonies will undoubtedly stir up in us a wide range of emotions; pain of course, but also fear, anger, shock, and a profound sense of frustration that these violations should persist some 45 years after the Universal Declaration of Human Rights." She went on to assert that the challenge confronting women is how to "translate emotions and passions into concrete practical actions."

The five thematic sessions of The Tribunal (Human Rights Abuse in the Family; War Crimes against Women in Situations of Conflict; Violations of Bodily Integrity; Violations of Women's Socio-Economic Human Rights; and Political Persecution and Discrimination), were introduced and moderated by women who have been active for many years in women's movements around the world and are leaders in the Global Campaign for Women's Human Rights. During the days preceding The Tribunal, these women also provided the testifiers with moral support and substantive advice on effectively presenting the testimonies.

In addition to Charlotte Bunch, *who moderated the final session on Political Persecution and Discrimination, moderators included:*

Monica O'Connor, *who is Training and Development Officer with Women's Aid-Dublin (Ireland) and has extensive experience working as a counsellor and policy advocate for battered women in Ireland, facilitated the session on human rights abuse in the family. In her introductory remarks, O'Connor spoke of how, "in Ireland as in many other countries, religion has been used to cast a cloud of secrecy and silence around the reality of violations suffered by women within the family." She expressed hope that the courageous testimonies delivered at The Tribunal would be a major step towards "lifting that cloud, so that we may all go back into the light and reality of women's lives."*

Nelia Sancho Liao, *a founder of the Asian Women Human Rights Council and longtime activist in the women's and democracy movements in the Philippines, moderated the session addressing war crimes against women. Her opening remarks focused on the military use of rape stating that "[w]omen in war are terrorized with rape. Soldiers rape to demoralize, to intimidate, to conquer in detention, in security zones, in front of family members....[E]xploiting rape in order to inflame conflict, exacerbates women's suffering. Rape in conflict routinely goes undenounced." Sancho Liao closed with a warning that "the failure to condemn rape and punish rape in war ensures that women will continue to suffer such abuse."*

The session dealing with violations of bodily integrity was facilitated by Gladys Acosta, *a long-time feminist legal activist from Peru who currently directs the women's human rights programme with Instituto Latinoamericano de Servicios Legales Alternativos (ILSA) in Bogota, Colombia. Acosta characterized the women's testimonies in this session as highlighting how "the limited human rights granted to women has resulted in violations of their physical space, their bodies, [and] their futures." She attributed the violations presented to the "impunity hidden in our moral and cultural frameworks, our laws and justice system" and cited them as examples of systemic "exploitation, oppression and discrimination perpetrated by our economic, political and social institutions."*

Florence Butegwa, *a lawyer from Uganda who is now the regional coordinator of Women in Law and Development in Africa (WiLDAF) based in Zimbabwe, moderated The Tribunal session on gender-based violations of socio-economic rights. In her introduction to the testimonies, Butegwa highlighted the impact of structural adjustment programmes (SAPs) on women's human rights, stating that "it is more difficult for women to have a job; it is more difficult for women to keep their job if they ever get one in the first place." These employment conditions become even worse when SAPs require states to drastically cut spending so that "millions of women in the countries where those programmes are enforced...no longer [have] free medical services" and "are forced to watch their children die." Butegwa cited an example of "one corporation in Africa, [where] the adjustment programmes required that the workforce be reduced by one half. That entire 50% of the workforce was all women."*

Although the testimonies were divided into five thematic sessions, the criticisms and concerns voiced by the testifiers were often interrelated. The patterns and similarities that emerged attested firmly to the indivisibility of human rights for women globally. The chapters in this section interweave and excerpt the words of the individual testifiers and the judges in order to present the major themes and concerns covered by The Tribunal. (The full transcripts of the 33 testimonies are available in Testimonies of the Global Tribunal on Violations of Women's Human Rights, *published by the Center for Women's Global Leadership.)*

Chapter 3
Human Rights Abuse in the Family

[T]he term 'torture' means any act by which severe pain or suffering, whether physical or mental, is intentionally inflicted on a person for such purposes as ...intimidating or coercing him [her]...for any reason based on discrimination of any kind, when such pain or suffering is inflicted...with the consent or acquiescence of a...person acting in an official capacity (art. 1)....Each State party shall ensure that all acts of torture are offenses under its criminal law. The same shall apply to an attempt to commit torture and to an act by any person which constitutes complicity or participation in torture (art. 4).

UNITED NATIONS CONVENTION AGAINST TORTURE AND OTHER CRUEL, INHUMAN OR DEGRADING TREATMENT OR PUNISHMENT

Everyone has the right to life, liberty and security of person (art. 3)....All are equal before the law and are entitled without any discrimination to equal protection of the law (art. 7)....Everyone has the right to an effective remedy by competent national tribunals for acts violating the fundamental rights granted him [her]....

UNITED NATIONS UNIVERSAL DECLARATION OF HUMAN RIGHTS

States parties to the present Covenant shall take all appropriate steps to ensure equality of rights and responsibilities of spouses as to marriage, during marriage and at its dissolution (art. 23).

UNITED NATIONS INTERNATIONAL COVENANT ON CIVIL AND POLITICAL RIGHTS

Women from Austria, Brazil, Costa Rica, Pakistan, Uganda and the United States opened The Tribunal with testimony about the abuse of women's human rights in the family. Several major themes recurred throughout their testimonies, including the universality of violence in women's lives; the fact that the "family" is not a site of safety for women; the connection between women's economic vulnerability and violations of their human rights; and the obstacles that prevent bringing "private" violations into public accountability.

The accounts of family-based human rights abuse demonstrated that while the forms of violence against women may vary with the cultural context, violence is an almost universal factor faced by women everywhere. Whether or not women become direct victims of gender-based violence, the systematic denial of women's socio-economic and cultural human rights, as well as political and civil human rights, leaves women vulnerable to violence, harassment, intimidation and economic dependence in their daily lives.

Numerous statistics are now available on the pervasive incidence of physical, sexual, emotional and economic abuse within family structures around the world. Women and girls are the predominant targets of abuses such as rape, battery, forced pregnancy, and incest—most of which are perpetrated by male family members in the home. The Tribunal testimony on this topic from every region of the world drew attention to the commonalities of women's plight in this, the most ignored sphere of human rights abuse.

Rosa Logar, coordinator of the Austrian Women's Shelter Network, cited several statistics on such violence in Europe. In Scotland, an analysis of urban police reports showed that 25% of all reported crime involved spouse abuse, making it the second most frequent offense.[1] According to the German magazine, *EMMA*, from October 1992 through March 1993, 124 women were killed in Germany, usually by a husband or a male acquaintance.[2] In all of Europe (not including the former Soviet Union) between 12 and 24 million women and girls are subject to violence annually, and there are currently between 800 and 1000 shelters and social institutions for abused women and children which house between 32,000 and 40,000 women and children on any given day. In Austria, Logar reported that 54% of all murders occur within families, with 90% of the victims being women and children. Logar characterizes the women behind these statistics as "refugees" who:

---

[1] Dobash, R.P. and R.E. Dobash. "The Importance of Historical and Contemporary Contexts in the Understanding of Marital Violence," 1976.

[2] *EMMA.* No. 2, 1993.

...escape during the night, without being able to take clothing or any other belong-
ings. If they are lucky they find relatives, friends, or shelters. If they are not they have
to return to their torturers. These women do not come from abroad; the circum-
stances they are trying to escape from cannot be called 'war.' These women are
refugees in their own country. They are not abused, tortured or displaced by 'the ene-
my,' but by their husband, boyfriend, or father. The place where everyone should feel
the safest, is the most dangerous for hundreds of thousands of women in Europe: it
is predominantly in their homes that women become victims of violence and in
most cases they become victims of their male relatives. Women are abused, threat-
ened, persecuted, and killed because they are women.

Stella Mukasa presented general testimony on violations of women's human
rights in Uganda, as well as recounting the particular case of Margaret Dravu, a
woman who continues to suffer the consequences of a domestic violence assault
in 1991. Regarding female human rights abuse in Uganda, Mukasa states,

Violations of women's human rights in Uganda occur at various levels. The viola-
tions range from traumatic cases of domestic violence, both physical and
psychological, to rape of women, defilement of children, and child marriages.
Notable and very challenging is the question of polygamy within the context of the
prevailing AIDS scourge. The situation is reinforced by issues like female circumci-
sion; lack of proper health facilities; nutritional taboos; early marriage and early
pregnancies; customs and cultural and religious practices which undermine
women's status, such as bridewealth; widow inheritance; and superstitions that vio-
late women's human rights in Uganda. The human rights of refugee women, as well
as internally displaced women, are also issues of concern.

Women are subjected to both physical and psychological violence, often by their
husbands, boyfriends, and even in-laws. The offenses of domestic violence and sex-
ual harassment are not explicitly provided for under the law, but are treated
generally as assault and battery under penal law. Due to traditional attitudes
ingrained in society, domestic violence is viewed as the normal wear-and-tear of
marriage, with the man having the rights to chastise his wife when he deems fit.

In a case reported in the papers in February this year, a man who was questioned
as to why he had chopped off the head of his bride when they had been married only
two weeks gave this reply: 'If you buy a cow and it misbehaves what do you do?' The
reply came from one of the spectators in a crowd: 'You slaughter it and buy another

one.' This sparked off roars of laughter, even among the police, who more often than not condone the crime and ignore it as a simple, private domestic matter. There is an urgent need to specifically protect women from such violations of human rights by placing domestic violence both on the world's agenda and in national legislations.

By demonstrating that the family is a place where the abuse of women and girls is commonplace, the speakers seriously challenged the powerful image of "the family" as a site of safety and nurturance. The testimonies reveal patterns of gender-based discrimination and coercion, in family structures and value-systems, that promote the disempowerment of women and foster disregard for their human rights. Gayla Thompson, an African-American woman living in the state of New York, USA, who testified to battery at the hands of her police officer husband, described the situation in the following way:

I married this man, but he beat me, he kicked me. He beat me bad enough to cause an abortion....I was able to get away at one point and call the police and when they arrived—because my husband was in his police uniform and had me on the floor kicking me and beating me and punching me—the other officers thought I was fair game and so they joined in....

I got to the point where I blamed my parents. I felt it was their fault because they never beat me as a child. My rationale was, 'Well, if you had beaten me as a child, I would have been able to come into this marriage and understand that beating was okay.' And when you are a Catholic, you tend to stay because it is part of your religion. You take on the vows of marriage and you really believe in your heart as a woman that, 'Well, it's up to me to make things work.' People say, 'Why did you stay? Why did you stay?' And you stayed because those are your duties and that's what you are supposed to do as a woman.

Perveen Martha from Lahore, Pakistan, described how her husband attempted to burn her to death:

I belong to a poor family....My parents arranged my marriage with Joseph, an electrician at the American Consulate in Lahore, on 10th July 1977....We are a Punjabi-speaking family but when I spoke Punjabi in my in-laws' house, I was ridiculed by everyone and developed an inferiority complex as a result....

My husband started to bring strange women to the house. When I tried to stop him he began to physically abuse me. I complained to his parents, but they only called me names and said, 'You don't fit into this household. Go find another place to live or else we will make sure that our son divorces you.' Thereafter, they started threatening me with all kinds of violence like, 'we will kill you or burn you to death.' I thought these were mere threats....After this I often suffered physical abuse at the hands of my husband and in-laws....I was not allowed to touch any household utensils. I had to start cooking my own food separately and keep my eating dishes separate....

Many times I was thrown out of the house by my husband or in-laws, but my parents would take me back and plead with my in-laws to let me stay....On February 24, 1984, while I was cooking food for myself, my husband Joseph began screaming at me. He picked up a gallon of kerosine oil, threw it on me, and lit the match.

Gabrielle Wilders, a Euro-American living in New Jersey, USA, and Sara Patricia Portugués from Costa Rica, both testified about their experiences of incest-rape. Their statements underscore the vulnerability of girl-children in the family structure. Gabrielle's father died in the Vietnam war when she was two years old, and her mother died of cancer when she was ten. Her step-father, a former-Catholic priest, fabricated an elaborate scheme of manipulation where he convinced Gabrielle that his repeatedly raping her was a form of "medical therapy" to prevent her from dying of cancer like her mother. This perpetrator's use of the family as a shield behind which to systematically violate her human rights, and the failure of various social institutions to question him, was a major theme in Gabrielle's account:

'Therapy' took place every night for the first couple of years. He gave me pills, which I later discovered were tranquilizers. Although I knew this 'therapy' was a sexual act, I believed this was a medical treatment that my life depended on....Regardless of being diagnosed as suffering from a sexually transmitted disease on several occasions, the medical community failed to investigate the cause....Throughout this time, I was frequently absent from school, my grades declined, and when present I cried openly in class. Despite the apparent signs of distress, nobody at the public school intervened.

Similarly, the testimony of Sara Patricia described a pattern in which societal blindness to the possibility of abuse within the family contributed to her victimization:

For many years, the fear of losing my father and my job made me remain silent. It was very difficult to accept that my father was the aggressor. Belonging to a society that does not protect me, I went to talk to a priest who advised me to pray for my sin. For a long time, I blamed myself and considered it my responsibility.

Several testifiers addressed how the particular position of women in the nexus of familial obligations exacerbated the impact of the violations they endured. Specifically, the primary responsibility of women for the well-being of children recurs as an important dimension in the abuse of their human rights. Different testimonies described how continuing to care for traumatized children serves as a constant source of guilt and a permanent reminder of the abuse. María Celsa da Conceiçao, from Brazil, testified as the victim of an attempted murder by burning at the hands of a boyfriend who refused to accept that their relationship was over:

Full of anger, he set my body on fire in front of my four year old son, saying that if I would not die I would look so physically injured that nobody would recognize me and no man would want me. I was very pretty and I was pregnant....Nowadays, I live in Rio de Janeiro with my son, who is a traumatized child with behaviour problems. This fact makes me very unhappy and guilty for he has been a witness to the crime.

Gayla Thompson explained it in this way:

When you destroy the life of a woman, if she has children, then you are also destroying the lives of those children so that you have a chain effect. Because of my depression, my son suffers from depression. I still have nightmares. I still have night sweats and I have lost my self-esteem. I, at that time, was studying the Russian language. All of these things I had hoped for and believed in were lost.

Separating women from their children adds yet another layer of difficulty to the lives of women who suffer human rights abuses. As Perveen Martha testified:

After some time had passed and my wounds had healed, it became clear that my face was fully burned and scarred for life. My husband refused to keep me in the house. He kept my children and told me to leave.

In addition to raising questions about dominant notions of the position of women and girls in the family, the testimonies also raise questions about how the family is understood in the broader socio-political context as the primary unit of the private sphere, where the actions of male heads of households are comparatively immune to outside scrutiny. These stories demonstrate that crimes such as marital rape, incest, battery, and other forms of violence in the family, are not just private matters that are too trivial to be treated as human rights abuse. In fact, the testimonies expose a pattern of human rights subjugation that includes the denial of "liberty and security of person," and actions that are forms of "torture" and "cruel, inhumane and degrading treatment" as specified in the *UN Universal Declaration of Human Rights [UD]*. Such human rights abuse demands an examination of the family as an institution which conceals the violation of the human rights of women and children and protects abusers from accountability.

The speakers also cited women's economic vulnerability as a major factor facilitating the abuse of their human rights within the family. In addition to facing economic discrimination in workplaces outside of the home, female family members routinely bear the brunt of the inequitable distribution of family resources within the home, and receive less food, less medical attention, and less education than male family members. Perveen Martha's account symbolizes the situation of complete female economic dependence, which is prevalent in developing economies and in industrial economies with high unemployment. Because their work is not valued in market terms, millions of women around the world are more vulnerable to human rights abuse in the family. They are perceived as economic liabilities both to their own families and to their in-laws. Gabrielle Wilders described the way in which her abuser exploited her economic dependence as a minor:

I frequently developed vaginal infections requiring medical attention. Since I depended on my step-father for transportation to, and payment for, medical care, I avoided telling him until I couldn't stand the pain any longer....After two years, I began to refuse 'therapy'....He countered by ignoring me, restricting my social privileges, and refusing to buy groceries.

María Celsa da Conceiçao described how, after 38 skin surgeries, she still faced discrimination in finding employment as a manicurist, her long-time occupation. Gender-based economic discrimination severely compounds violations of women's human rights in Europe as well. As Rosa Logar noted:

Women cannot leave violent men because they depend on them financially and have no alternatives. In Austria, the average salary of a woman is not high enough to pay the rent of an apartment. Women's shelters are often the only places where women find protection and support. But there are not enough organizations. Many of these institutions exist only because of the commitment and the unpaid work of other women. The financial resources of the shelters are still insufficient. In a small town in Upper Austria for example, the society to protect animals gets more public financial support than the [women's] shelter... Not only violence itself, but also its consequences are relegated to the 'private' sphere, and the cost of the consequences have to be borne by the victims themselves.

Finally, the women testifying repeatedly demonstrated that even when they had overcome the many obstacles to bringing the so-called private violation to the public space of accountability, justice was rarely served. Most often, women are informally obstructed in their efforts to secure their human rights through national procedures. As Gayla Thompson described it:

The police department wiped clean all of the letters I had written, the complaints I had filed, and, because [my husband] was a police officer, I was told I could not prosecute. I was not able to obtain an order of protection. I was unable to get anything. My attorney never went to court for me. I was suicidal.

In the case of Margaret Dravu in Uganda, no effort whatsoever was made to seek justice. During one of the frequent attacks levied against her by her male partner, Mr. Nkoba,

[He] grabbed her, beat her up and kicked her after which he threw her onto the lit lamp. Beside the lamp was a plastic can which was set on fire, causing burns all over Miss Dravu's body. She ran out of the house in flames and began to roll on the ground. When the flames were out, Mr. Nkoba picked her up, rushed her to a nearby hospital and left her there.

Yet, more than two years later, Nkoba has not been apprehended or his whereabouts located. In fact, around the world it is the perpetrator of the violence, rather than the victim, who is favoured by the legal system. Perveen Martha's husband initiated divorce proceedings based on a groundless allegation that she had committed adultery. As a result, she can now be prosecuted on criminal charges under Islamic law, and will have to fight a difficult battle if she is to gain custody of her children or financial support from her husband.

In some circumstances, women did manage to get their cases addressed by the judicial system, usually with the support and backing of women's organizations. While this was clearly a victory of sorts, the outcome of the cases generally added to the human rights abuse already endured by the women. María Celsa da Conceiçao described the judicial process when she called on a women's police station in Brazil:

When I left the hospital, I was surprised to learn that my former boyfriend was free and that the police had not registered the crime. I looked for a women's police station, and only then, did a police enquiry begin. It looked like the law was going to be put into action, a prosecutor (a black man who had understood my case) and the judge who had heard my story recommended jail as his punishment. However, a new prosecutor and a new judge entered the case, and they started to depart from the terrible facts. Both proceeded to evaluate my life instead of judging the crime committed against me. My aggressor was absolved of all guilt. The justice system has considered this case closed and there is no way to modify their decision.

Even where victims of human rights abuse successfully see their abusers punished by the legal system, the results can be less than satisfactory. As Gabrielle Wilders described:

[A] psychologist's evaluation of my step-father [classified]...him as a 'sadistic, manipulative, compulsive and repetitive child molester'....In the end, my step-father pleaded guilty to 2nd and 3rd degree assault and was sentenced to 7-9 years incarceration at a treatment facility for sexual offenders. He was released from the facility after a mere 18 months....[I]n a civil trial, I was awarded $200,000 dollars...to this date, some nine years later, he has only paid $10,000.

By highlighting the prevalent reality of human rights abuse without redress in the private sphere of the family, the testimonies underscore the gross inadequacies of an international human rights system which has focused almost exclusively on state-sponsored violations of narrowly-defined political and civil rights.

The testimonies also demonstrate the repeated failure of legal and judicial systems around the world to ensure that cases of family violence are prosecuted and justly sentenced, and that women are protected from violence throughout these processes. Such systematic failures reflect the denial of both "equal protection of the law..[and]..the right to an effective remedy by the competent national tribunal"

(*UD*, arts. 3 & 8), and are evidence of a failure to abide by the mandate "that the competent authorities shall enforce such remedies" *(UN International Covenant on Civil and Political Rights [ICCPR]*, art. 3(c)). The testimonies show that the lack of national-level redress to violations of women's human rights within the family stems from gender-based discrimination in legal and judicial systems globally, which in effect compound women's human rights abuse through the denial of their civil and political human rights.

Judge's Statement: The Honourable Elizabeth Odio

I would like to thank Charlotte and all those responsible for this event. However, I think that they made a mistake by inviting me. I was not born to be a judge. They are objective and impartial; I am neither objective nor impartial when dealing with the pain of my sisters. I am sorry if I disappoint some people. After listening to all these testimonies, we, the ones who came to this Conference representing our governments with new approaches to human rights issues, ask ourselves, "what are we doing at this World Conference?" Maybe I could contribute some reflexions to the official Conference, but this forum does not need my contribution.

Since 1945, after the second World War, states have had responsibility for the respect of fundamental human rights and are submitted to international vigilance. In the *UN Universal Declaration of Human Rights* of 1948, it is stated that human beings are born free and equal in dignity and rights. Furthermore, article number one states that everyone "is endowed with reason and conscience and should act towards one another in a spirit of brotherhood."

This international dimension of human rights was a consequence of the tragedies of the war, like the holocaust, which demonstrated the incapacity of states to guarantee respect for the human rights, the absolute rights, with which every one and each one is born. The creation of the international community was a way to guarantee respect for these rights. Since then, many international mechanisms, like the *UN Convention Against Torture and Other Cruel, Inhuman and Degrading Treatment or Punishment*, have been created.

Still, there is a "trap" from which we have not escaped. When the family is defined to be behind closed doors, we go back to the old Roman version of rights, in which rights within the family do not get publicly discussed. From the door through to the inside of the house, rights are governed by the father's rule, and we have not progressed beyond this point.

What we need to do about this "trap" is to make the international community understand that men and women must work toward the elimination of the absurd discrepancies between private and public rights.

It is important to remember that in the *Convention Against Torture*, we define torture to be acts that carry intention to cause pain, suffering, and intimidation. This definition can be applied to each and every testimony that we heard today. The state and the international community cannot remain absent.

In thinking about why violence against woman inside the family has not found international and national answers, in order to understand this violence, we believe we must consider three fundamental notions of our societies:

▶ An idealized vision of the family which ignores hierarchy and supports a comunity based on interests;

▶ The view that women do not need protection inside the family, an old Roman notion; and

▶ The idea that abuses of human rights cannot happen in the private sphere.

The elimination of this opinion is our major goal today and in the following years. All these notions contradict our reality, a reality represented by these seven testimonies which can be generalized to the whole world. When we talk about this reality, many would say that there is juridical support for these problems in the internal legislation of each country, and that each nation does protect women. This way of thinking supports the idea that violence against women should not be considered a violation of human rights.

However, we listen today to testimonies from the whole world showing that national legislations do not give answers to violence against women, that we women do not exist, and that abuses against us are defined under legal codes but are not considered crimes in practical life. Yesterday, I read an article in a Spanish newspaper saying that rapes inside marriage are not considered crimes. This example typifies women's situations inside states and under internal judicial codes. This is the reason we must struggle for the recognition that violence against women is a violation of our fundamental human rights.

This Tribunal is only the beginning of this struggle and next year, when the UN will be celebrating the International Year of the Family, let's keep in mind what we heard today when people talk about family rights.

Chapter 4
War Crimes Against Women

[Women as protected persons] who at any given moment and in any manner whatsoever, find themselves, in a case of conflict or occupation, in the hands of a Party to the conflict or Occupying Power of which they are not nationals...shall be especially protected against any attack on their honour, in particular against rape, enforced prostitution and any form of indecent assault. [Furthermore, with respect to non-international conflicts,] outrages upon personal dignity, in particular humiliating and degrading treatment, rape, enforced prostitution and any form of indecent assault [are also prohibited].

FOURTH GENEVA CONVENTION

...[G]enocide means any of the following acts committed with intent to destroy, in whole or in part, a national, ethnical, racial or religious group, such as a) Killing members of the group; b) Causing serious bodily or mental harm to members of the group; c) Deliberately inflicting on the group conditions of life calculated to bring about its physical destruction in whole or part...(art. 2).

UNITED NATIONS CONVENTION ON THE PREVENTION AND PUNISHMENT OF THE CRIME OF GENOCIDE

War and its dangers are endemic around the globe. Since the end of World War II, major or minor conflicts have embroiled some part of the globe all the time. According to Mahbub ul Haq, author of the United Nations Development Programme's annual *Human Development Report* (1993), twenty-two million people have died in more than 120 conflicts during the so-called peaceful transition since 1945. Despite the beginning of a "new world order," there are few signs that war and conflict are decreasing. Persistent struggles within national boundaries as in Palestine, the Sudan, Nicaragua or Northern Ireland, and, more recently, the ethnic conflicts in the former Yugoslavia and the former Soviet Union have focused international attention on internal conflicts and instability.

Wherever it occurs, war has a severe and dramatic impact on the human rights of women. The Tribunal testimonies on "War Crimes against Women" suggest a pattern that is repeated through time and across cultures and geographic regions. Any number of conflicts might have been selected to represent the impact of war on women's daily lives. The speakers' accounts addressed Japanese crimes against women in World War II, the ongoing conflicts in Palestine and Peru, as well as more recent sites of upheaval including Somalia, the former Yugoslavia, and Russia. Three major themes emerged from these testimonies: women's bodies are figuratively and actually the site of combat in wartime; women's human rights are violated through the exploitation of familial relationships; and, women suffer disproportionately from economic and social dislocations caused by conflict. Yet, despite the devastating impact wars have had on their lives, the speakers reveal women's strategies of resistance and resilience in the face of war and demonstrate the imperative of involving more women at the highest level in securing peace.

In all conflict situations, women's bodies are used as the figurative and literal site of combat. Of all the metaphors used by politicians, propagandists, and journalists to describe military attack, rape is one of the most frequent. These testimonies demonstrate that rape and violence against women are often integral aspects of military strategy and the inevitable consequence of the gendered logic of conquest in all conflict situations. Chin Sung Chung, who works with the Korean Council for Women Drafted for Sexual Slavery by Japan, gave the following background to the experience of the so-called comfort women during World War II:

When the Japanese Imperial Army rampaged the continent of Asia at the beginning of the 1930's, it started to establish army brothels. After Japan invaded China in 1937, this practice was systematically perpetrated in almost all Japanese Army garrisons, including Manchuria, China, the South Sea Islands, and even in Japan and Korea. It is estimated that some 200,000 women were registered as sex slaves for the Japanese Army.

...[T]hese women were mostly young girls under 20 years old, forcibly detained from Korea (80-90%), with others from China, Taiwan, the Philippines, Indonesia and even European countries. Some were kidnapped while drawing water from a well or working in the field, [and] others were induced by officials of the colonial government to be employed in Japanese factories with good pay. All those young girls left home without imagining that they would be the comfort women of Japanese soldiers. Most of them were raped on the way to army brothels.

Bok Dong Kim, a survivor of sexual slavery in Japan, gave the following account of the war crimes committed against her:

My older sisters, all being of marriageable age, got married quickly to avoid being taken away by the Japanese military. As I was the fourth daughter and only fifteen years old, everyone assumed I would not be detained. Thinking I was only a young girl, I went around freely, even taking the cow out to graze. But they came asking for me....One day, the official came with a Japanese person and said, 'You have to go with Chong Shin Dae'....In those days women could not read, so my mother conceded to the demand believing what she was told, that I would have to work in a factory and would be free after three years.

Moved from one location to another for several months and living a relatively normal life, Bok Dong Kim was not overly concerned until she arrived at Guangdong where she reports:

[A]s soon as we arrived, military doctors gave us a full check up. It was a venereal disease check. To take my clothes off and expose previously unexposed parts of my body in front of an unknown man, to spread my legs to a military doctor, and to lie there on the table made me extremely afraid and wonder what this was all about.... at that time at sixteen years of age you knew nothing and were really a child. I did not even know what a man was. To prevent the examination I kicked a lot, but saying it was compulsory, they forcibly removed my clothing and carried out the checkup.

After the examination, we were taken to the Comfort House. The Comfort House was an empty fifteen story building. On the first floor were soldiers and on the second floor was the Comfort House.... From the second day they forced us into full-scale comfort work, servicing the soldiers. At the beginning, I resisted receiving men. For this, they didn't give me food and beat me. I could not continue to refuse. Thinking, 'even if I resist I am hurt,' I decided to do as I was told. But, good grief, I could not endure this sexual victimization having had no experience of men. My internal sexual organs were torn and swollen. I cannot explain this suffering. Even speaking about this fact is humiliating. My only thought was to escape or die. But I could not escape.

There were many women at that place. We were not allowed to gather together but were divided in different areas. The Comfort House was located outside the army base. Ordinary soldiers would come out at 8 o'clock in the morning and went back in at 17:00. Two hours later, the higher officers came out. On week days, I received usually about fifteen men. From Saturday to Sunday it was terrible. On week days there was time to sit and relax, but on Sundays it was unspeakable. They came in and went almost straight back out, and then the next one came in, and the next person, and so on. It's impossible to remember how many soldiers came in. It was tens of soldiers. Maybe more than fifty. When each soldier came in, he carried a small ticket and a condom. In the evening I would take the tickets to the administrator and he would check them off.

Today, more than 50 years later, similar accounts of imprisonment and rape are emerging from the current war in the former Yugoslavia. As Aida Zaidgiz, who is from Sarajevo, expressed: "When I heard Chin Sung Chung, such an emptiness entered my soul because what happened over 40 years ago, what happened in Japan, is happening right now." According to a 1992 report of the School of Medicine at the University of Zagreb:

at least half of people detained in camps controlled by the Bosnian Serbian army were women and about a third of them were obviously raped; therefore one can estimate that there were at least 10,000 raped and tortured women until now...[and] official sources from Bosnia and Herzegovina claim that according to their evidence the total number of women raped is even higher—estimates ranging up to 60,000 raped women.

Fadila Memišević, from Bosnia-Herzegovina and a member of the Zenica Documentation Centre of War Crimes, gave the following statistics:

Zenica is the centre of the free Bosnian territory and the largest group of Bosnian-Herzegovinian refugees is located there. Approximately 80% of them are women. Of the former total of 2.4 million Muslims, only 750,000 now live in this country; 250,000 were killed and over one million were expelled and scattered all over the globe. Our centre's data bank contains documents on 20,000 'disappeared,' 50,000 killed or injured children, 40,000 raped women and also on 1,350 people strongly suspected of having committed war crimes. But these figures are not final. They are amended daily and are presently increasing rapidly. And they are not merely statistics. This information is based on testimonies of expellees who can be named.

While rape and forced pregnancy have been used on the largest and most systematic scale against Muslim women as part of the Serbian policy of ethnic cleansing, women of all nationalities are victimized by the sexual violence of war. Aida Zaidgiz recounted the following stories showing the impact of these policies on women:

Susanne is the daughter of a Serb mother and a Muslim father. When the human rights violations, these horrible things done to Muslims in every place occurred, she resisted. Therefore, she was taken to a rape camp. And now in Zagreb, we are dealing with a woman, her name is Ayse. I got to know her at Betchowa hospital. She was eight months pregnant (as the result of rape)....All the time she felt she would go crazy, she insisted that she would give the baby away, she didn't want to have anything to do with it and so forth. And then when she delivered, the child was born dead. I talked to her and she was really depressed. I tried to tell her 'somehow you didn't really want it.' But she responded, 'I carried it for nine months under my heart.'

There is a lot of sorrow in the world and we have to start doing something about it. At this moment, in Bosnia/Herzegovina, every 1.7 seconds a Bosnian Muslim woman, a Bosnian Serbian woman, or a Bosnian Croat woman, with the emphasis on Bosnian, is raped....And we're always talking about the victims. But all of us avoid naming the perpetrator. Because it is against the perpetrator we have to fight.

Lepa Mladjenović , a founder of the SOS Hotline in Belgrade and of the Women in Black anti-war opposition to the Serbian government, spoke of their work with women war victims:

We have listened to our Bosnian sisters and heard their silence.
We have heard their need for our solidarity, they speak out with their bodies.
Some of them cannot say anything at all.
Some of them were as young as 15 years old.
Some of them recognized soldiers as their neighbours.
Some of them (Serb) were systematically raped in (Muslim, Croat) soldiers' barracks.
Some of them (Serb) were raped by the soldiers of the same (Serb) nationality.
Women of non-Serb origin (Muslim, Croat, mixed), raped by Serb soldiers, who came for abortions in Belgrade, felt horrible pressures, and were avoiding communication with us, or we never met them at all.
Some of them told us stories about other women who never survived.
Most of them we met were pregnant, waiting for abortions or birth, and none of them we spoke with wanted the child.

Some of them told us about women's solidarity across the nationalities.

...Finally, we have learned that this war is another occasion in the history of genocide rapes. We are witnessing thousands of Muslim women being subjected to systematic rapes, death, and deportations as a part of the genocidal military tactics (ethnic cleansing) of the Serbian Army. We therefore demand that genocide rape be named as such, and that political and military Serbian leaders be put on trial for that crime.

A frequent sub theme expressed by the women who testified on the use of rape in war was the intense shame and the fear of being ostracized by their own communities. Unlike men who, in times of war, are often publicly valorized for the violence they endure (or commit) for their country, the violence levied against women is either made invisible or is seen as a source of shame for the women and as a reminder of the conquest of the nation. In the aftermath of World War II, Bok Dong Kim described her situation:

When I returned home, I was 23 years old. Having left at 16 years old, it had been eight years. My older sisters and younger sister had all gone to Japan with their families, and only my mother was left, alone, keeping the house at Yang San. After I had gone, many others had also been taken away. Because we all kept it inside, I don't know who had gone to the Comfort Houses. They all just said they had been working in factories or hospitals. In fact, I also said I had been at the 16th Military Hospital all the time....[A]t first even my mother didn't know my secret. Because she kept on talking about trying to marry me off, I told her. So then my mother gave up on trying to make me marry.

...There were girls from our group in Tong Yong and in Ko Jae. Those girls hadn't learned anything else but this foul work, so many fell into prostitution....[A]fter a bit I met an older man whose marriage had failed and we got married. My husband didn't know about my history either. It's now five years since he died. I feel sorry for him. I could not bear children, so he died without even one child to follow on.

Slavica Kušić of the Centre for Women Victims of War in Zagreb, Croatia gave the following account of how shame affects the women there:

Hidajeta is a young mother of two. I have been helping for months to conceal her identity in the refugee camp. Her sin was that she believed that by testifying against the atrocities in the detention camp where she was held, she would help the world to discover how deep the crimes are, to stop them and to punish the criminals. It happened that journalists sent her story around the world and left her to live or die her life alone. She is hiding from the rage of other women who were together with her in the camp. The world saw their stories and they realized the help of the world is nonexistent and their 'shame' is great. The surroundings further this shame of being raped. So they hide this 'shame.' They don't want to admit they were raped or to give birth to their unwanted children.

In the former Yugoslavia, some women have sought to deal with such abuse of rape victims and the use of the rape of women for nationalistic purposes through female solidarity across ethnic lines. As Lepa Mladjenović described it:

We are witnessing many different misuses of the women raped in war. The Serbian government (and not only the Serbian) is using the fact of raped women to increase the hatred against the enemy and to rationalize their national chauvinism. Some journalists have been putting enormous pressure on women raped in war. They were using them to promote their media companies....Different state institutions manipulate numbers to such an extent that one has an impression that they are glad to increase the numbers. They use these as weapons against the enemy, and they never point out the reality of male violence against women in their reports....

War rapes did not become a media issue because people were interested in protecting women's rights. But it is up to us now to use this break in the invisibility of rape in war to censure male violence against women. It is up to us to continue our group work with women survivors in solidarity with each other's pain, trauma, isolation, and loneliness. Because many women told us how they escaped prisons and death by being helped by women of different nationalities, they taught us once again that solidarity can save our lives and that women's solidarity is a force that men do not count on.

Many women's groups, such as the Korean Council for Women Drafted to Sexual Slavery by Japan and the Centre for Women War Victims, are working to secure justice for women whose human rights are violated in the interests of war. Chin Sung Chung describes the challenges faced in this process. When World War II ended, she notes:

[A]llied western nations didn't force Japan to pay reparations...because the nations in Asia were too weak to demand such reparations. It was also because the United

States wanted to stabilize the capitalist system in Asia quickly, and thus adopted generous policies to Japan after the war. In regard to the comfort women case, it was not until 1991, after the excavation of army materials laid bare the truth, that the Japanese government admitted to the systematic operations of exploiting comfort women. The Japanese government is still reluctant to look into its own historical files, and attempts to silence this heinous wartime crime against humanity...by offering a meagre amount of money without admitting legal and moral responsibility.

Japan has begun to send its...[f]orces to Asian countries in the name of peace-keeping operations, and is also trying to become a permanent member of the UN Security Council. We are very concerned about the latest developments created by Japan....Without sincere repentance for the past crimes against humanity, and due steps for the reparations, how can Japan contribute to peace in Asia and the world?

....If the world does allow Japan's current moves without judging its war crimes, it may condone recurrences of such atrocities in the future. Now we are witnessing the tragedy of collective and premeditated rape in Bosnia, another example of the world's irresponsibility when faced with such crimes.

Slavica Kušić's closing remarks reflect similar concerns:

The Centre for Women War Victims demands the following: First, that the war should be stopped and all detention camps closed. Second, that war criminals should be tried and punished. Those who started the war and those who carried out the atrocities themselves should be declared war criminals. Those who have carried out the atrocities should be tried in the place where the crimes occurred because that is the only way that innocent people can live together again.

Women are also victimized through the exploitation of familial relations as a war strategy. For example, women are often forced to witness the brutal torture and/or murder of loved ones as a means to instill a general sense of terror in the community under attack. Slavica Kušić related the following account:

Her name is Minka. She is 14 years old. Not a woman, not a little girl. The horror that she has experienced has made her face a stone mask. She watched out of the bushes, where she was hiding with her mother and her brother, as her father was murdered. They killed him and then cut him in pieces with a yard axe. When there was calm again in the village, they emerged from the bushes to bury their father and then continued on foot into the unknown. Now they are waiting for a third country to grant them exile, even if only temporary. Minka wants to go back to her village to be present at a trial for war-criminals, because she saw them and knows their names. She went to school with their children. One of the men was her teacher.

Similarly, women's usual position as the primary caretakers of infants and young children, makes them vulnerable to forms of psychological torture if their children are also victimized. Slavica Kušić told "Hirzeta's" story:

On the next bed in the barracks was Hirzeta. She has not been able to sleep since she came to the refugee camp. The nightmare that would haunt her in her sleep would be to go back to the place where she left her four month old baby alive. She was fleeing from her village where her home was burning. She was carrying her four month old twins in her arms, travelling by night and sleeping in the shelters of the second World War. When her energy was finally drained, she was faced with the decision to die and therefore leave her sons to die or to choose one and save him with all her remaining energy. She left the younger one, born five minutes later, with a pacifier in his mouth and a note with his name on it. She said that she left him and that Allah will help him. On that spot her memories stopped.

Women who try to respond to the needs of their communities are often abused by both sides in internal conflicts. Ema Hilario is an indigenous leader from Peru who organizes women in the shanty towns of Lima. The terrorist group, Sendero Luminoso (Shining Path), continues to target her as an ideological enemy for her efforts to improve women's daily lives. As a means to incite terror throughout communities in Peru, such women activists and their family members are being murdered and tortured. Ema Hilario gave the following account:

Then, December 20th, six people—five men and a woman—came to my house pretending to be people who sell bread. At this time, my brother-in-law was visiting me, and he was the one who opened the door. He received six shots; one in the mouth, one in the face and the rest in the other parts of the body. Only two bullets were taken out; the other four are still inside his body. After him, it was my husband, who was also shot, and still today he has a bullet in his back. I was paralyzed with fear, I could not move. I was on my bed, it was six in the morning. Then I turned my head up, and I saw this man holding a tommy gun and saying that I had not fulfilled their demands because I continued to look for ways to become powerful. Then I pro-

tected my head with my hand against the first shot, the second, the third, the fourth, the fifth, and the sixth. My bed seemed to be shaking. I was listening to the shots and thinking that they were killing my children and my father, who was 80 years old. I then pretended that I was dead. My face was all bloody due to my arm, and thanks to it I am alive. After 10 minutes, my house was silent. Forty bullets were found around my house.

Many women suffer disproportionately under wartime economic, social, and political dislocation. Both the immediate graphic violence of war, and the longer-term societal destruction which results, are experienced in gender-specific ways by women in their daily lives. Olga Kudryavtseva, a Russian photographer, presented a photographic documentary of the on-going war in the Caucus mountains which has received scant international attention:

The sides in this conflict are two Russian Republics, North Ossetia and Ingushetia and two autonomous Republics, South Ossetia and Georgia. Today, because of the violence and conflict, more than 15,000 people—both Ossetians and Russians—are homeless and are not safe. As a result of the fighting and the violence in the Vladikovkaz area in the six months between November 1992 and March 1993, more than 40,000 people have become refugees, 316 are lost, 331 killed, among them 140 Ossetians and 179 Ingush. Almost 4000 houses have been burned and destroyed.

In this part of the world, I see bloodshed, people dying, mothers suffering, children as orphans. The cruelty and revenge is growing. The pictures you see are of women and children. Women have been tortured with knitting needles, and severed women's heads were attached to armored personnel carriers. Scalps taken from people who are still alive, and women's breasts are put on tanks.

Even when world media choose to make a conflict situation visible internationally, the gendered dimensions of the war are rarely considered. Janet Tello presented the case of Sandra Gonzáles who was denied a just legal process having been kidnapped, raped and battered by government workers in the context of Peru's current civil war:

In a society surrounded by political violence, sexual violence is not perceived. It is tolerated and considered of no importance. The non-existent response of the state to this problem makes the state responsible for the impunity of the violators and worsens the already critical situation of Peruvian women by producing a new layer

*of violence in Peru. Between 1981 and 1989, more than 70,000 cases of sexual vio-
lence against women were reported to the police. These figures show that political
violence is accompanied by an escalation in sexual violence.*

In addition to the increase in rape and violence directed against women in war
situations, the economic upheaval, destruction and poverty caused by war domi-
nates women's daily lives. Ema Hilario's story exposes the multiple layers of
human rights violation experienced by women living in war zones:

*In 1988 I was arrested because I had started to mobilize against the high cost of food,
against unemployment, and to find means for the farmers to improve their produc-
tivity. Due to this movement, the police arrested 200 women and I was among them.
They maltreated me. I was so badly beaten that I had to have an intestine operation.
At this period, the country was in an unrecognized civil war. In 1991 we suffered as
women. ...[T]he Shining Path were trying to control the women's organizations. They
were against popular organizations of women. They killed many women as a way to
create fear and terror. It is why I say that we, with our organizations, are in the middle; we suffer violations of human rights by the state through the armed forces and
also through the weapons carried by the Shining Path.*

Fadila Memišević also described the impact on women of the destruction of
the social and economic infrastructure that results from war:

*In Bosnia-Herzegovina, every woman is now a war victim. Because of their children,
mothers are under constant stress. It is a skill to survive—without electricity, water
and basic food stuff—in a desperate effort to feed the family. Women who were
working are now in a waiting position. All production has been stopped or drastically reduced. Schools and universities are closed. Besides the population, this war is
also destroying the education system. The schools are destroyed and used as refugee
camps. In occupied areas, schools have become concentration camps in which mass
rapes and maltreatment are on the daily agenda.*

Randa Siniori presented testimony (prepared with Rana Nashashibi) describ-
ing the position of Palestinian women in the context of military occupation and
nationalist conflict. They underscored the invisibility of violations of women's
human rights in conflict situations, as well as the ways in which the goals of the
nationalist forces do not include the improvement of women's lives as women:

In the occupied Palestinian territories, violence against Palestinian women exists in a variety of forms: at the national level by Israeli occupiers, based on our national identity; within our society, because of patriarchal practices and because of the fundamentalist movement; and within our homes.

As Palestinian women living under occupation, we face violence at the hands of the Israeli occupier. All Palestinians are subject to the violence, but Palestinian women also face threats of torture, blackmail and repression. Sexual harassment, insults, and intimidation are a part of daily life for many since the perpetrators usually are soldiers manning look out posts on the roofs of Palestinian homes, driving in military jeeps throughout villages, and shouting curses through loud speakers.

Under the occupation, all Palestinians face daily infringement of basic human rights....However, rarely in Palestine do we associate human rights violations with such issues as physical, sexual or psychological abuse. We tend to think of human rights violations strictly in terms of the infringement of our national rights as Palestinians....

Over the past four years of the Intifada, our women's movement has matured and learned a great deal. We have learned that achieving statehood will not necessarily bring about social change for women. Our women have contributed and struggled hard during the Intifada, but we haven't felt that the social issues so important to us and to our rights were met seriously or accepted by the leadership as a whole.

Asha Samad from Somalia pointed out the hypocrisy and passivity of the international community in its acceptance of gross human rights violations as part of the culture in countries like Somalia. She stressed how the exclusion of women from the decision-making and peace negotiating processes fosters more war and destruction, in addition to violating women's human rights:

You see the Somali women as victims of war and conflict. Indeed, that they are. But they also are the ones most potentially able to be the peacemakers and the developers of their country.

The people making war during the colonial period or during the present period are not the women. The people forming armies, exploiting foreign aid, and giving foreign aid to countries that have been documented as terrorist states, are not the women. The people picking up the pieces, the people being raped, sexually and otherwise physically harassed, yes, we are the women. Those in the refugee camps are almost all women and children. Those suffering harassment, not only in Somalia, but when they are escaping the country into some neighbouring countries, are the women. Sometimes, the police of those countries, and other men from their own country and from those countries, often also take advantage of their impoverishment. When they are trying to get food for their children, or for other people who have survived with them, when they're trying to get legalized status in the neighbouring countries or in developed countries, too, quite often men have to pay bribes, and women have to pay with sex.

Asha Samad also discussed how cultural and religious institutions compound the human rights abuse experienced by women in conflict situations:

Men and women are born into a clan—a patrilineal clan, of course—and they stay in that clan. That's their clan of birth and death. However, women quite often marry into another clan, which is fine in peace time. But when there's war, they may have to choose between the clan of their birth, that is of their father and brothers, or the clan of their husband and their children. What a horrible choice! There have been many cases where women were married for many years and had children; when war starts, they're considered a fifth column, spies within the homes of their husbands who are told to divorce them and send them out, (not with their sons of course, the children stay at their father's side). They're just sent out because of the attitude, 'we can't keep you, you're an enemy within our house.' Can you ever imagine such a state?

It happens quite a lot, so women have more at stake in wanting peace, and lose more in terms of war.

Judge's Statement: The Honourable Ed Broadbent

I am the first man to have spoken today, and before I make comments of a particular nature on the series of grotesque events we've heard described to us, I want to say that I am not ashamed but I am deeply saddened. I'm not ashamed because like the other men here, and the men attending meetings upstairs presumably, we didn't commit these vile acts that we've heard about. But I am deeply saddened, almost beyond description, because as one of those who spoke said, and I quote her, 'those making the war are not women, those doing rapes are not women, however those being raped, yes, we are the women.' And although these unspeakable acts have been committed by individuals, often men deranged in a personal way, probably a large majority are the results of not years but centuries, not of one culture, but of almost all cultures around the world, of patriarchy, of conditioning that has caused men, at best, to view women consciously or unconsciously as second-rate citizens, and at worst, as disposable chattel.

The second point I want to make about men: I look around this room, and I think of my work, as a man, who has a responsibility for a human rights centre, who in recent months has been in Guatemala, El Salvador, Kenya, Europe, Thailand. I have met with individuals in those countries, and we have talked about the right of association, we have talked about the right to form a union, we have talked about the right to form political parties, and we have talked about the right to speak out freely. At all those meetings there were men and there were women. But I look around this room, and I ask you to look in your aisle from one end to the other, and notice the gender. We have a session here, in which we have heard abominable testimony of incredible cruelty, and I ask myself, when we are talking about the rights of women, where are the men?

I'm not making a glib judgement here, because it is a complex matter of conditioning. But at some point, it is the responsibility of the leadership of human rights institutions and organizations throughout the world to recognize that, yes, there are important civil and political, cultural, social and economic rights that belong to all citizens, men and women, but that there are a number of evil, abominable violations of rights that are exclusively inflicted upon women, and we must pay attention to them.

After having heard from the victims here—courageous, moving, passionate women—I want to make just a few points. First of all, these acts we've heard about in times of war, to put it in technical or legal language, are breaches of the Fourth Geneva Convention. That is a formal way of saying that rape, forced prostitution, and forced pregnancy are forms of torture. We must understand legally and morally that they are forms of torture, and we must respond that way.

I want to add one word about Burma, because our Chairperson said that the women of Burma had wanted to be heard, and they aren't here. Well, I was in Thailand just a few months ago, and I was at a camp on the Thai-Burma border. I walked down the path of this camp, which is a nine year old refugee camp built in 1984, with children running all over who have no other existence but growing up in that camp, and I walked into one of the huts. I saw a teacher there who had been translating for us earlier, and she said, come in. I went in and I met a young woman who was 20—the same age as my daughter. And she told me what had happened to her in the previous six weeks: she had been in her village over the border in Burma, and it had been overrun by the Burmese army who had killed some men, forced the other men out, and then taken women prisoners. And she was among them. For about a month, she was forced to be a porter during the day, carrying military supplies and food for this detachment of the Burmese army. And during the nights, each night for a month, along with other young women, she was systematically gang-raped. She put up with this for a month, and then she walked for 10 days to get to the border, to get to the camp. She had to flee her own country; she went over the border to get to safety. So that is what is happening to many women in Burma.

And it's happening, as we've heard today, in other countries, in one former country less than an hour's flight from where we are today. Such violent treatment of women must be seen as a violation of human rights. We must understand it, we must condemn it, we must prosecute it, and we must stop it.

The second point that I want to make is that such acts, in formal language, are crimes against humanity. And why are they? Technically, again, because of the severity of violence and persecution based on gender: selected, targeted persecution. The victims we have heard about today were selected because they are women. Such rapes have been used as an instrument of ethnic cleansing. We should call a spade a spade, and report evidence that has been conveyed to us. Some of us came of age during the second World War, and as a Canadian, I came of age hearing of ethnic cleansing of a different kind in the Germany of the 30's. Well, ethnic cleansing and forms of genocide were wrong in Germany in the 1930's, they are wrong in the former Yugoslavia, they're wrong in Burma. Ethnic cleansing and that form of murder is a technical violation of law; they are crimes against humanity which must be stopped.

The third point I want to make is that such crimes against humanity must not be simply understood, recognized, and documented; they must also be prosecuted. As we just heard, the women don't want vengeance, they want justice. Those responsible, those who believe abominable breaches of the Geneva Conventions can be ignored must be taught a lesson. War crimes committed must be war crimes prosecuted. Justice made available to the claims of men in the past must be made available for the rights of women today. It might be put this way: gender-free justice is, after all, the only kind of justice.

The last point I want to make is that I hope the women upstairs at the governmental meetings, who are out-numbered ten to one by men, are listening. But they must not only listen, they must also start to understand. And because they have the power, they must now act.

Chapter 5
Violations of Women's Bodily Integrity

No one shall be subjected to torture or to cruel, inhuman or degrading treatment or punishment. In particular no one shall be subjected without his [her] free consent to medical or scientific experimentation (art. 7)....No one shall be held in slavery and the slave trade in all its forms is prohibited (art. 8).

UN INTERNATIONAL COVENANT ON CIVIL AND POLITICAL RIGHTS

No one shall be subject to discrimination by any state, institution, groups of persons, or person on the grounds of religion or belief (art. 2).

UN DECLARATION ON THE ELIMINATION OF ALL FORMS OF INTOLERANCE AND DISCRIMINATION

Forced prostitution is a form of slavery imposed on women by procurers. It is... the result of economic degradation that alienates women's labour through processes of rapid urbanization and migration resulting from underemployment and unemployment. It also stems from women's dependence on men....Sex tourism [and] forced prostitution...reduce women to mere sex objects and marketable commodities (para. 290).

THE NAIROBI FORWARD-LOOKING STRATEGIES FOR THE ADVANCEMENT OF WOMEN

The first two segments of The Tribunal—on Human Rights Abuse in the Family and War Crimes against Women—illustrated some of the ways in which women are routinely subjected to battery, torture, rape, and mutilation both within their families and in conflict situations. The women testifying on Violations of Bodily Integrity expose how patterns of coercion and violence against women permeate broader social, cultural and economic institutions and practices aimed at controlling women's sexuality and reproduction. Testimony of women from Canada, the Netherlands, Nicaragua, Peru, and Sudan highlighted four major themes: International economic and structural upheavals are resulting in the proliferation of new or revised forms of sexual and economic exploitation of women; Violations of women's bodily integrity are often defended or excused in all parts of the world in the name of cultural or religious practice and expression; Women's human rights abuse as the result of forced conformity to heterosexual norms is pervasive; Women who are physically challenged, or disabled, face additional gender-specific socially constructed obstacles to the realization of their human rights.

Upheavals in both economic and political systems have had gender-specific ramifications, often adding to women's vulnerability to sexual and economic exploitation. Lin-Lap Chew works with STV (Foundation Against Trafficking in Women in the Netherlands), which gives assistance to women in the sex trade who have been brought there from other countries, primarily Asia and now Eastern Europe. She gave the following background to the growth in trafficking in women from Central and Eastern Europe (CEE):

In the six years that STV has been working professionally (since 1987) we have given assistance to more than 400 women. This is but a small number of the women who have been 'trafficked' into the Netherlands. Field workers, health workers and police estimate this number to be between 1000 and 2000 per year....The traffickers use various methods. We have assisted Polish women who have answered advertisements for waitresses and cooks, and who have instead been put to work as striptease workers and forced to sleep with customers. We have assisted Bulgarian women who had been kidnapped in [the former] Yugoslavia and who were then held prisoner in a flat and brought to work in a window on Amsterdam's famous 'wallen' (prostitution area). We have worked with Ukrainian women who were forced to work because they had signed IOU's for loans with multiple interest rates which they would never have been able to repay if they went home, and so were forced to work as prostitutes. And we have assisted Russian women who said they had been induced into prostitution by the KGB and the 'mafia.'

The women from Central and Eastern Europe had many things in common. They were relatively young: the youngest we have met is 16 and the average age of those we helped is 23 years. Most of them have had at least basic education, some have had professional training and some, third level education. They were invariably from urban areas, and many had jobs in their countries, albeit for very low wages. Undeniably, all of them left their countries willingly and eagerly, when the opportunity presented itself....

The fact that women from CEE are being trafficked to almost all regions of Europe should not surprise us. The same dismal conditions of failing economy and fruitless and unending political and social upheavals are the motivating forces behind BOTH the flight of those who seek opportunity as well as the unscrupulousness of those who find opportunity in the desperation of others....

Lin Lap Chew recounted the following testimony on behalf of Grazyna from Poland whom STV has been helping. It both illustrates how women's economic vulnerability fosters violations of bodily integrity and highlights the gender-based human rights abuses which affect immigrant women in particular:

My name is Grazyna. I am 30 years old and I come from Poland. I used to work in the ship-building industry, but since the so-called revolution there is no more work for me. The economic crisis has turned my life upside down. I am divorced, and I have two children.

In September 1991, I had been working in a restaurant in Yugoslavia [when I]...met a man, John G. He asked me whether I was interested in going to work in a restaurant in Germany where I would earn three times as much as in Yugoslavia for the same kind of work....A few days later, he introduced me to another man, Robert, who said that he was the manager of a restaurant in Germany.... A few days later, Robert came with two other men to fetch me. There was another woman with him who was also going to work in Germany. At the German border, I had to give him my passport because he somehow convinced me that it was better if he was the one to hand it to the immigration officers. He never gave it back to me afterwards. On the way we stopped at a hotel somewhere in Germany. Robert and one of the men, Mario, stayed there with me, and the other man went with the other woman somewhere else. There they told me that I had to work as a prostitute. I protested, but to no effect. When I kept on refusing, Mario raped me while Robert took photographs. He threatened to send the photographs to my mother if I continued to resist. I became very frightened after that. I was afraid that my mother, being a staunch Roman Catholic, would get a heart attack if she saw those photos. Then we drove on to Essen. There, I was sold to a third man, Josef. Later I discovered that Robert had

received Dm3000 from Josef for me. Josef brought me to the Netherlands.

In the Netherlands I was forced to work as a prostitute in a 'window,' in a street full of prostitute windows. ...They also said that it was no use going to the police, because they were paying the police too. I had to earn at least 600 guilders per day. If I did not earn enough, I was beaten. They beat me on the head and kicked me in the belly. I still suffer pain from this mistreatment. They showed me guns and said that they would not hesitate to use them if I did not cooperate. They would throw my body in the canal and no one would be able to identify me.

I was terrified. I was sometimes allowed to keep some money. Then, I sent the money to my mother and children in Poland, but did not dare to tell them of my predicament....I pretended submission, worked and laughed in the hope that my captors would relax their guard and that I could avoid any more physical assaults. I was still determined to escape. Finally it worked. In an unguarded moment, I fled without knowing where to go....

[Eventually] I was interviewed by the contact officer for the Ministry of Justice. I told him how I had come to the Netherlands, how I was forced to work as a prostitute. I told him I was afraid to return to Poland because I feared that the traffickers might take revenge on me for running away, and also because of the compromising photos that Josef had made. But the Ministry of Justice decided that I did not fulfill the criteria for recognition as a political refugee, and rejected my request for asylum.

Luckily my lawyer...contacted the Foundation Against Trafficking in Women (STV). They explained about the laws against trafficking in the Netherlands and told me what my rights were as a victim of trafficking. Since I had nothing more to lose, and I was terrified that Robert and Josef would look for me, I decided to press criminal charges. STV contacted the anti-vice police, but strangely to me, the police did not believe me. They thought that I had made up the charge of trafficking after my asylum request had been rejected, so that I could stay in the Netherlands. They could not understand why I had not filed the trafficking charges in the first place.

Again I was fortunate. In another city, the woman with whom I had been brought to Germany had also been brought to the Netherlands and had also filed charges against Josef and Robert. The police in that town had contacted STV for assistance for her. Finally, my case was taken seriously. This gave me some sense of security, and it also meant that I would be allowed to stay in the Netherlands until the case had been tried in court and all judicial procedures were ended.

Violations of women's bodily integrity are frequently normalized, excused, and even defended in the name of the cultural or religious practices and expression of a particular group or country. Examples of this occur in many different forms around the world, including forced pregnancy in Catholic states such as Ireland and Malta, the stoning or burning of women who allegedly commit adultery under some interpretations of Islamic law, and dowry traditions which foster vio-lence against women in some Asian countries. Nahid Toubia, a medical doctor from Sudan, testified about female genital mutilation (FGM) which is often defended and protected as one such cultural right:

I stand here today to testify on behalf of many girls and women who had no choice when parts of their bodies were removed in the name of culture and social confor-mity. I testify for all the women in all cultures, East and West, who undergo the physical pain and psychological agony of bodily manipulations to conform to the prevailing social requirement of femininity. In my society, that means cutting out essential parts of the genitals of women. And because they are women, their fate is to marry, give their husbands sexual pleasure, and give birth to many children while suffering in silence, obedience, and acceptance.

Because as women we are made economically and socially powerless, most of us have little chance to say NO to stop the injustices imposed on us by society. But today, many of us have found our voices and are speaking out against a custom that abus-es and humiliates us. We will no longer be intimidated by accusations of disrespect to our culture.

Our cultures are already changing very rapidly, and not always in positive ways. Much of what we inherited was positive, but we must be honest and admit the neg-ative aspects. Today, our traditional ways are being undermined by materialism and greed, which seem to be embraced with little objection. It is only when women want to bring about change for their own benefit that culture and custom become sacred and unchangeable. As women, we too have the right to decide what parts of our culture we want to preserve and what we want to abandon....

Female Genital Mutilation is not a private issue nor a concern of one nation. It affects around 100 million women who live in 26 African countries, a few minorities in some Asian countries, and immigrants in Europe, Canada, Australia, and the United States. Every year, around two million girls are at risk of being subjected to this cruel and unnecessary tradition....I invite you to come and sit with me in the outpatient Obstetrics and Gynecology department of Khartoum Hospital, where I worked for many years [and where] hundreds of thousands of women pass through with chronic complaints all metaphorically related to their pelvis. They complain of headache, fatigue, loss of sleep, backache, and many other vague symptoms all uttered in monotonous depressed voices. Probe them a little, and the psychological pain and anxiety over their genitals, their sexual lives, their fertility and other complications of their circumcision come flooding out. These women are holding back a silent scream so strong it could shake the earth....

Nahid Toubia quoted Asma El Dareer, a Sudanese physician who conducted the first national survey on female genital mutilation:

I was circumcised in 1960 at the age of 11. I remember every detail of the operation and the worst part was when the wound became infected... When I was 18, it was the turn of my younger sister. I was totally against her circumcision. My father wanted the milder type (the clitoridectomy) but my mother insisted on the severer type (the infibulation). Eventually, my sister had the intermediate type, virtually the same as infibulation. The suffering of my sister made me hate circumcision even more than my own earlier experience.

Asma Abdel Haleem, a human rights lawyer and Islamic scholar from Sudan, was also quoted:

With regards to female circumcision, it is important that there be a final religious announcement clearly stating that it is a form of mutilation and therefore forbidden. It is not sufficient for religion to shun the practice. Religion should be used as a tool for condemning and preventing its occurrence. The participation of women in the reinterpretation of religion will be crucial.

Nahid Toubia made the following suggestions for eradication of female genital mutilation and the alleviation of its affects:

1. It must be stated in the relevant conventions that FGM and other cultural practices that interfere with women's bodies and personal integrity are violations of human rights and all concerned governments must be persuaded to ratify them.

2. All professional organizations must pronounce it unethical for any of their members to undertake circumcision of a girl under the age of consent. They must help train their members on how to provide safe, supportive, and respectful health services for women who already have been circumcised.

3. International health and development agencies, as well as national governments, must commit funds to programmes to educate and counsel people against FGM.

4. At the appropriate time and in consultation with women's groups and national human rights and legal bodies, laws should be passed to prohibit the practice.

Another pervasive source of women's human rights abuse which takes a variety of forms globally is forced conformity to dominant heterosexual norms. As Randa Siniori stated in her testimony about women in conflict situations:

Throughout our work with Palestinian women, we have found a common denominator in almost all of the women's lives. Women are forced into doing things against their wills, coerced, if you like....from being forced to leave school at an early age, being forced to wear a veil, having to marry before she's ready or being forced to marry someone she does not want, to being forced to have children.

Women's attempts to resist such coercion are often met with a wide spectrum of human rights violations from discrimination and harassment, to violence and death. While enforced heterosexuality is used to control women of all sexual orientations, lesbians pose the most visible and profound challenge to this coercion and are therefore often explicitly and legally persecuted by their families and communities, in work places, and as part of state policy. Rebeca Sevilla from Peru, co-chair of the International Lesbian and Gay Association, gave the following personal testimony and account of the persecution lesbians face in every region:

I come from a male chauvinist country. In general, it is a very difficult process to identify myself with the word lesbian—to be able to ignore the pejorative context of this word. I come to give testimony about the difficulties and the persecution that affect our lives as lesbians. I am speaking out in order to make visible a pattern that affects many absent sisters and many who are present here today...

When I was 23, I had my first relationship with a woman. We stayed together no longer than three months. It was very hard for me. When it was over, I tried to forget, as if it were a mistake in my life. I decided to go to a therapist to ask for help. I then started to look for a boyfriend....[and] I forced myself for many years to be someone that I was not and did not want to be. It was a difficult situation and I could not share it with anyone.

I then developed a relationship with another woman. But I still had not resolved in myself the realities of my situation. Simple things like introducing someone as my girlfriend; taking her hand in a public area and expressing our affection is difficult for us lesbians to do. I worry about hurting my mother, our mothers, friends, and co-workers. I recognize that for many years I lived a secret, lying to myself like many other women. I was afraid of losing study and job opportunities, afraid of being rejected by my family and friends, or even by my girlfriend's family....

Many times lesbians, gays and other sexual minorities are considered sick persons who need treatment to become normal again. Our mental health is exposed to strong emotional strain due to the daily negative responses we receive and the extreme social and/or familial repression....We lesbians are victims of persecution, coercion, and illegal arrest, and our personal security is constantly threatened. In some countries, the incidence of violence and murder related to sexual preference is extremely high. In Brazil, data collected by the gay group from Bahia indicates that over the past ten years 2,000 murders of gay people were registered. This is only a partial indicator since the information is restricted to cases reported by the media. In 90% of the analyzed cases, the crimes have not been resolved and the aggressor remains free....

Marly's case is an example of this impunity. She is from the city of Maceio. In 1983, she was raped with a bottle and killed with her lover Rita da Silva. The aggressor was a member of her family and he remains free. This is only one of the faces of this "social cleansing" that drives the physical extermination of lesbians, gays, prostitutes and street-kids....Where "permits to exist" are doled out, where we are invisible as lesbians, where we ourselves don't see how our human rights are devalued and unknown, where we don't have control over our bodies and lives, where we don't have access to an independent economic life, women are denied the status of personhood.

Despite changes toward the end of the 20th century, heterosexuality remains the only valued social option. In terms of sexual politics, we can say that we live in a totalitarian regime, where only one model is respected. We demand and claim the right to control our bodies, we want to have the right to live with dignity, we want to be able to organize our families with children in liberty. We also want to be able to enjoy our capacity to love as lesbians.

A fourth area addressed under the rubric of Violations of Bodily Integrity was the position of women who are disabled. Although the term "disabled" has been subject to much criticism when used as an adjective to describe individuals who are physically challenged, the testimonies in this area reframe the issue by illustrating how societies create the conditions of disability by causing actual physical damage and/or disempowering individuals who cannot do certain physical things like walk or see. Further, disability takes on certain attributes in relation to gender, class, geography, and ethnicity.

Women are particularly vulnerable to violations of bodily integrity in the area of reproductive health. In every region of the world, women often only receive regular health care in connection with contraception, pregnancy, and childbirth. The treatments are often invasive or unnecessary, potentially injurious, and frequently do not occur with women's informed consent. As a result, women's human rights are violated around the world through procedures related to reproduction and population control, including forced pregnancy, coerced abortion and sterilization, unsafe contraceptive devices, unnecessary hysterectomies, and the incompetent use of epidural anaesthesia and episiotomies. Petrona Sandoval's experience of becoming paralyzed as the result of medical intervention during childbirth in Nicaragua underscores both the gendered and the North-South dimensions of the construction of disability:

I used to work as an auxiliary in an infirmary until the tragic day of March 3, 1986. On this day, in order to save my life and the life of my baby, I was submitted to a Raquida anaesthesia in my spinal column. This is an anaesthesia applied in every country, called epidural anaesthesia. It is used to obtain a regional neural block in the body....Eight days after the anaesthesia, I started to have strong pains in my spinal column. The doctors said that it was a normal reaction to the anaesthesia. Two months later, I started to fall down all the time for no reason. This process continued for four years until I ended up sitting in this wheelchair....

The number of victims in Nicaragua is not known since it is not reported to the health centers. We believe that the number of women in this situation is around 500....Many patients arrived at the assistance centres who were subjected to the [epidural procedure, and] many of them, due to ignorance or lack of opportunity or information, do not report the negative consequences of their operations. A study by a Swedish agency estimates between 600 and 2000 cases in Nicaragua. Despite the fact that this situation has persisted for ten years, the Nicaraguan government and the international health community have failed in their role. This situation has never been concretely investigated, and as a result of that, we still do not know the cause of it. Among the theoretical reasons for it are: inadequate hygiene; the use of contaminated syringes and/or anaesthesia; expired medications (which is the most likely explanation); and, inadequately equipped people (...Nicaragua suffered a blockade and the people who work at the health centers were working with their hands only)....

Johanna Gilbert from Canada, who uses a wheel chair, told her story of coping with a degenerative back condition which affected her after she had sustained severe injuries through an attack by a male acquaintance. Following an evening out drinking with this man, Johanna Gilbert was sexually assaulted and severely battered by him:

This is the beginning of my nightmare. I was in a state of shock. I had a lot of pain in my back....I remained at the hospital for two days in observation. At the time that I left, because of my state of shock,...I didn't realize what had happened. Two weeks had passed before I decided to file a complaint. Since they could not protect me 24 hours a day, I decided to move. Still today, I live in fear because the aggressor is free and he keeps harassing me.

After that comes a process that lasted for one and a half years. The judges were changed five times, for reasons that I don't know...I was humiliated [and felt] I was judged because of my physical appearance....The defense lawyer had tried many times not to consider my testimony since I had been under the effect of alcohol....

The nightmare continues with the physical, psychological, and financial damages, and the end of my dreams: to have children, to marry, to be [financially] independent. [I live with] the frustration of my physical condition after many surgeries, an atmosphere of indifference, and also my physical condition keeps deteriorating. I need to face the reality that I depend on others all of the time.

Gilbert's account has much in common with the testimonies on Human Rights Violation in the Family where the women spoke of the physical disability which often accompanies domestic violence. On behalf of Margaret Dravu, Stella Mukasa described how,

Since the [domestic violence incident], Miss Dravu has always had difficulty with eating. She has undergone four surgeries so far but she still is finding it difficult to use her hands. Yet, she has to fend for her four children.

Petrona Sandoval's testimony also emphasized how women, who are already physically challenged on some level, are further disabled in gender-specific ways by socio-economic values and institutions. As she described it, her testimony:

Is a call from hundreds of women who are affected...in Nicaragua. It is also a warning to all the nations of the world that women's rights should not continue to be violated as has happened in my country where our rights are violated every minute....Examples include the denial of our right to have as many children as we want since our spines cannot support a pregnancy; the right to work with dignity, since many of us were professionals before and today we are not accepted anywhere; we are single mothers, since in many cases husbands abandoned the wife as soon as she was confined to a wheelchair. The society surrounds us with walls where we do not have any opportunity of integration with others. We feel like parasites.

To end, I ask your solidarity with the handicapped women in our fight to demand recognition of our existence as women wronged by a discriminatory system. We have demanded just compensation from the health ministry but we have not received an answer. We have also demanded medical treatment and the provision of adequate means to recover.

In the name of all my friends who are also handicapped, and in the name of all the Nicaraguan women who, in one way or another, have had their rights violated, I say that the struggle against the violation of our rights has only started.

Judge's Statement: Justice P.N. Bhagwati

Madam chairperson and friends. The testimony of these remarkable women, who have boldly come forward to give evidence before us about their traumatic experiences, has been moving and heart rending, and it shows that violations of bodily integrity against women, which seem to occur in all parts of the world, are brutal, systematic, and structural. These atrocities are an affront to the basic human dignity of women; they are often justified by reference to cultural norms and practices and misinterpretation of religious and other traditions. As one of the presenters pointed out, religion needs to be reinterpreted in the light of revealing human rights norms. The testimony addresses trafficking in women, rape of disabled women, genital mutilation, persecution of women because of their sexual choice, and denial of women's rights to health, including reproductive health care services and information.

These testimonies provide evidence of great violations of women's human rights, which are conferred in the many national constitutions and international as well as regional human rights conventions. But merely confronting rights is not going to help. These rights will remain merely paper documents, what I call paper tigers without teeth or claws, unless there is general desire on the part of the state and the people to enforce them. We often find a lack of desire on the part of the state to enforce these human rights of women, largely because—I believe almost principally because—the state agencies are also dominated by males. Male domination is so strong and powerful that these laws, which should be enforced in favour of women, are not really enforced as they ought to be.

We recognize these abuses of bodily integrity and dignity of women as gross violations of women's basic rights, and they deserve the strongest condemnation. Whatever there might be in religious or cultural traditions or practices in a bygone age must not be allowed to justify violations of basic human rights of women, because these human rights are universal in their application to all human beings, irrespective of their race, language, gender, colour or religion. These human rights inhere in women, as in men, by virtue of their being human, and they cannot be denied on any ground whatsoever. Women are the victims of unjust cultural and religious practices and traditions, and it's high time that we stop these practices and traditions which are sanctified in the name of cultural or religious norms and practices. These instances of violations of human rights which have been presented before us are not stray incidents, but they are typical of the kinds of violations which are taking place against women in all parts of the world. Such violations need to be addressed and remedied at all levels: national, regional, and international.

Every effort has to be made by national governments, the United Nations, and specialized agencies to immediately take steps for various purposes: Firstly, recognizing abuses of bodily integrity and dignity, even if they take place in the home, as violations of women's human rights. Secondly, preventing such abuses and violations through effective implementation of human rights instruments; gender sensitive education and training to create human awareness; empowering women to use these instruments for vindication of their rights; and eliminating promptly the root causes of such abuses and violations, which attempt to justify themselves on the basis of misconceived religious, cultural and other traditions, including stereotypes which assign inferior and degrading roles to women to the detriment of their dignity and health. Thirdly, undertaking of a massive campaign for bringing about human rights awareness and attitudinal changes in the thinking of men vis à vis women and their human rights. Unfortunately, I must share the regret expressed earlier that I see very few men here. I think it is necessary that more men hear these stories so that they can be educated. I think men need to be more aware, and to be educated more about these things, than women, because women are the victims and it is the men who are the perpetrators of these atrocities.

Another measure that needs to be taken is to encourage and strengthen women's human rights groups so they can participate actively in all matters relating to promotion, protection, and enforcement of women's human rights, and fight for such rights. An example is what has been done by Nicaraguan women, as presented by Petrona Sandoval. It is really necessary to provide easy access to justice for redressing these abuses and violations through adoption of innovative strategies. As was evident from the testimony given before us, it is necessary to bring about changes in the legal system in order to make it more sensitive to violations of women's human rights.

Today, the legal system appears to be heavily weighted against women; it is male-dominated and there is a bias. Judges, therefore, have got to be oriented towards gender justice. We often hear the myth that judges are objective, impartial, that they only administer the law; they are not concerned with persons behind the cases that come before them. This is a myth which has been nurtured by the male tradition. When cases come before the judges—and I'm speaking as a judge—the judges have to see who are the persons behind it; here, they are helpless women demanding justice from the court, and the court can't shut its eyes to the dictates or demands of justice and merely rely upon so-called 'blind paper law.' The judges have definitely got to be sensitized so they will realize that what they have got to do is justice, and not merely administration of the law. The judges must not be blind to the violations of women's basic human rights, and therefore they have got to keep their eyes open to see the misery and suffering, the pain and anguish of battered, violated women, and to try to wipe the tears from the eyes of a fellow human being. These are some of the things that are essential, but these violations of human rights of women are the most despicable examples of what I call masculine bestiality.

Some of the instances which have been conveyed to us by these last five witnesses clearly show how men have behaved in order to incapacitate women, in order to make them disabled, totally oblivious to the fact that they are also human beings. They seem to be treating women as a commodity for their sexual pleasure. They forget that women are also human beings with a heart, with a mind, with emotions and sentiments. Have they not the right to claim happiness? Merely because they are born as women, have they forfeited the right to happiness? Why is the misery and suffering which we have seen today typical of misery and suffering taking place everywhere else? Why does it not bring tears to our eyes? Why does it not invite the wrath of the society? Why do we ignore these things? These are the questions which have been posed by these witnesses who have given evidence before us. I am sure that women's power will develop, and one day, not very far from now, all of these injustices and atrocities will be swept away.

Chapter 6
Socio-Economic Violations of Women's Human Rights

Everyone as a member of society, has the right to social security and is entitled to the realization, through national effort and international cooperation..., of the economic, social and cultural rights indispensable for his [her] dignity and the free development of his [her] personality (art. 22)....Everyone, without any discrimination, has the right to equal pay for equal work....Everyone has the right to a standard of living adequate for the health and well-being of him[her]self and his [her] family, including food, clothing, housing and medical care and necessary social services...(art. 25).

UN UNIVERSAL DECLARATION OF HUMAN RIGHTS

Further, no one shall be required to perform forced or compulsory labour (art. 8)....In those states in which ethnic, religious or linguistic minorities exist, persons belonging to such minorities shall not be denied the right, in community with other members of their group, to enjoy their culture, to profess and practice their own religion, or to use their own language (art. 27).

UN INTERNATIONAL COVENANT ON CIVIL AND POLITICAL RIGHTS

All peoples have the right of self-determination. By virtue of that right they freely determine their political status and freely pursue their economic, social, and cultural development....In no case may a people be deprived of its own means of subsistence...(art. 1)...[These] rights...will be exercised without discrimination of any kind as to race, colour, sex, language, religion, political or other opinion, national or social origin, property, birth or other status (art. 2).

UN INTERNATIONAL COVENANT ON ECONOMIC, SOCIAL AND CULTURAL RIGHTS

The *Universal Declaration of Human Rights* clearly states a commitment to socio-economic rights, but this has rarely been met at the international level. To the extent that it is taken seriously, it has usually been framed in terms of the rights of trade unions. While trade union organizers are often subjected to human rights violations, with women organizers being persecuted in specific ways, unions themselves are generally male-dominated, market-centred, and have failed to take account of the gendered dimensions of socio-economic rights. For example, rarely do women receive more than 70 percent of what men earn for comparable work. Women face discrimination in education, sexual harassment in the work place, and are relegated to low-skill, low-paid job markets. Vast numbers of women work outside the market in their homes, in agricultural production, and in the so-called informal sector for little or no pay, and their contribution to the economy is not counted as part of the Gross National Product. Further, where women are part of a non-dominant community or group which is economically marginalized and discriminated against, they experience gender-based violations of their socio-economic rights through a filter of racism and/or colonization.

This context converges with both an increasing global trend toward female-headed households and the prevalence of value systems that place the responsibility of childrearing with the mother to create tremendous economic hardship for women as a group. This hardship itself constitutes a pattern of gross human rights violation and, in addition, fosters vulnerability to further violations, including forced prostitution, forced emigration and illegal status, violence in the home, poverty, disease and malnutrition, and the denial of the right to education.

The women who testified in this section addressed these issues through accounts of: socio-economic violations against migrant women; the situation of indigenous women in the context of human rights violations against their group; human rights concerns affecting both women who organize in trade unions and the women they represent; and, the human rights implications for women of structural adjustment policies. These testimonies of women from Bangladesh, Barbados, Cape Verde, the Philippines, and the United States (Native American) reveal that immigrant women, indigenous women, women in poverty, and women workers across the globe have severely curtailed access to legal, monetary and institutional resources in their daily struggle for human dignity. In the face of present and future economic restructuring, this marginalization constitutes and compounds the denial of their human rights.

María Lourdes de Jesús, who is from Cape Verde and now lives in Italy, testified to the human rights violations she experienced as a migrant African woman in Europe:

I first migrated to Lisbon, Portugal at the age of 12, when my mother thought that to help I must follow what my other compatriots have done. 'For a better life,' she said, but it was not like that. Using my minor status as an excuse, my pay was very low, although I was working like an adult. All the while I was sending money to my mother. I was exploited working as a domestic helper with a family for three long years.

Her testimony also explains, in general, the situation of the growing numbers of 'third world' female domestic workers in Europe:

As of today, the story of the so-called Third World migration to Italy has been analyzed as male migration. The statistics, though, reveal that 50% of these are women, and a good part of these migrants come from Africa, the majority of whom are working as domestic helpers. Because of the kind of work they do, these women have been 'invisible women'....

It is difficult to document the violations [against migrant women] for various reasons, including the fact that many of the violations occur within private homes where migrant women fear losing jobs, or are ashamed and embarrassed to talk about experiences which they would prefer to forget.

One Cape Verdean woman was only able to avoid being sexually harassed by her Italian employer by locking herself inside the bathroom; she escaped in the middle of the night when he was sleeping. There are also cases where women suffer sexual assaults in silence to avoid being fired from work. Others who were not able to endure the provocation were forced to leave their jobs. Another situation of exploitation is the trafficking of young African women for prostitution. Young women who do not control their lives work as prostitutes under miserable conditions, and receive only some money out of their earnings from the pimps.

She noted that most migrant women are employed as domestic workers.

This work involves several serious limitations to freedom. A domestic worker has only two afternoons free per week, yet she cannot choose the days she wants to be free. There are scarce opportunities for her to interact with the social reality in which she lives. She has few available occasions to establish social relationships or to give a sense of continuity to her life. Language problems and self-expression lead to difficulties for her in communicating in other social spaces and personal spheres. Limitations to personal intimacy and the lack of autonomous living space for domestic workers lead to a sense of frustration and the sublimation of affective needs. They also lead to the impossibility of living with her family, with a husband/partner and children. [A migrant woman also experiences] problems of low self-esteem, which causes her not to believe in her capacity to improve herself and her relationships with others....

[In general,] African women in Europe suffer a triple discrimination: living in a continent where women are not emancipated and where power is dominated by men; as foreigners who find difficulty in having their rights respected; and simply for the colour of their skin.

Another focus of the testimonies in this section of The Tribunal was on the experience of indigenous women. Bernice See, an Igorot woman living in the Philippines, addressed the connections between the ongoing socio-economic marginalization of indigenous peoples and violence against indigenous women:

Igorots consider wife battery to be a public crime which can be resolved in the indigenous socio-political structures....Wife battery merits banishment, divorce, the breaking of the peace pact, or severe fines and an oath not to do it again under pain of banishment. That is why there have been very rare cases of domestic violence in our traditional societies. However, these systems are slowly losing their usefulness as villages are integrated into the market economy, as christianization proceeds, and as the state imposes a legal system which does not recognize customary law as part of jurisprudence. Thus, increasingly, the supports available to Igorot women are slowly being eroded, leaving them more and more vulnerable as cases of domestic violence increase. The cases of domestic violence we are seeing now are occurring among younger couples and among women married to non-indigenous persons, like myself....

This violence has cost me a lot. Ten years ago, I left a promising teaching career in the university because I felt I was not going to be an effective teacher. Who would want to have a teacher who is sporting a black eye, or whose jaws have become the colour of eggplant due to battering? Who would want to employ somebody who is absent when needed because she has to take time to heal herself? As feminist activists, we must look into the socio-economic dimensions of gender violence. How many opportunities have been passed up by us victims because physically, mentally and psychologically we cannot go to work? How many contributions have been lost because we had to take time out to heal ourselves?

Bernice See also places this rise in domestic violence in the context of militarization and destructive economic development policies which amount to a "Total War Policy" against indigenous people in the Philippines:

We are being bombed, starved, killed. We are hamletted in places we cannot call home. We are forced to leave our homes, fields, and worship places. We cannot go to our fields and swiddens because we might get killed, raped, molested or harassed. Or because a curfew has been imposed on us. Or because our crops have been destroyed by the bombs and bullets, or helicopters landing on our fields....

In our experience, militarization and development come together. This is because we have conserved our resources through the ages through our environmentally-sound resource management practices. Our territories are now what is left to be tapped by government and big business....This is development aggression.

The structural violence also has a gender-specific impact:

Women's organizations, including barrio (neighbourhood) health committees which are female dominated, are ordered to be dismantled. Socio-economic projects like village cooperatives with as little as US$10 in capital have to suspend operations, or else what little goods they have will be confiscated. Training and education activities to empower women have to be canceled.

Women leaders are summoned for military interrogation and visited several times in their homes to explain why they are linking up with NGOs. After three months, they undergo the same routine because of change of command.

...Cases of gender-specific violence have been documented and published. Rape, gang rape, attempted rape and sexual molestation by military and paramilitary personnel are occurring...Take the case of Delia: Delia Mangay-ayam was a 24 year old teacher in the provincial centre. On the February 3, 1991, four men entered their home and robbed them. They dragged Delia out and serially raped her. She was able to identify one attacker, which led to his arrest. Delia filed a case of robbery with multiple rape against this attacker and another one who was arrested later. Under suspicious circumstances, the first suspect was able to escape from custody. On June

19th, four months later, three men again went to Delia's home, got her and her father out, serially raped her, and then killed her and her father. Delia had 15 gunshot wounds all over her body.

Charon Asetoyer is a Native American activist who lives on the Yankton Sioux Reservation in South Dakota. She described the structural violence confronting Native Americans in the United States which manifests itself in chronic health problems within the Native community:

Health care is a right that is guaranteed by treaty.... However,...[t]hrough constant financial devolvement at the Washington, D.C. level, the annual budget of the Indian Health Services, which provides basic clinical care, only provides surgery for people whose life is in danger. This means that a...condition that...would normally require surgery for a person to live a healthy life must wait until that person is dying...before surgery will be done. That kind of health practice increases the chances of a person dying from the complications of the surgery and minimizes recovery....

Alcohol has often been used to occupy, divert and make vulnerable Native people in order to take land, minerals, and other possessions. This practice is still [prevalent]. At the local level in our community, the township of Lake Andes is run by white merchants. The local liquor store is owned and operated by the city of Lake Andes, South Dakota. The store allows Native people who are on public welfare and Federal welfare to charge alcohol up to the amount of their monthly check.

At the Federal level the Indian Health Services has never developed a proper health-oriented or socially appropriate response to the alcohol problems for Native people, and especially for Native women. Fetal Alcohol Syndrome (FAS) is the leading birth defect for Native babies. FAS is an irreversible birth defect caused by a mother drinking alcohol during her pregnancy. It is totally preventable. Currently, there are few if any treatment centers that will take pregnant Native women who are chemically addicted to alcohol beyond the seventh month of pregnancy.

As in the testimony presented by Bernice See, the human rights violations committed against Native American people as a group are experienced in particular ways by women, as Asetoyer reports:

On a daily basis, women's rights are denied. The right to health care, access to it, police brutality, violence against women, and that double standard that exists in the court system when Native women try to use it to assist them in prosecuting their perpetrator, are the most harmful violations experienced in our communities by Native women....

Each year, thousands of Native women are sterilized. And most recently, with the new hormone manipulation contraceptives such as Norplant and Depo-Provera, the Indian Health Services is targeting our women for their use. There is little regard given by the Indian Health Services—[a Federal agency]—to the health of women when considering the use of these methods of contraception. The goal is to reduce the risk of a Native woman giving birth to another Native baby. As of the most recent Government census done in 1990, there are reported to be less than two million Native Americans in the United States of America....

Currently, there is a movement on reservations to arrest pregnant Native women who are drinking alcohol and to put them in jail. Yes, this will stop them from drinking alcohol, but there are no medical or prenatal services for the women once they have been arrested. This practice has its own set of problems, and can put both the mother and child at great risk of dying.

Ayesha Arshad, a union organizer and garment worker from Bangladesh, addressed human rights violations facing women workers and women union organizers:

In Bangladesh, as in other countries of the Third World, women and women workers in particular, suffer inhuman exploitation. The economic exploitation of their labour and patriarchal oppression result in severe violations of women's human rights. Many women workers are forced to work until 20:00 hours daily. There is no provision for rest, for transport to the workplace, for medical assistance, or for childcare. Women are rarely able to obtain their legal entitlement to maternity benefits. We are also denied access to legal protection of our rights.

The situation of women working in rural areas is even more desperate. Women are involved in a range of occupations, including construction... but in every area they are denied fair wages. In all these cases, their human rights are being violated. The IMF and the World Bank dictate our official policies.

Ayesha Arshad recounted the human rights violations she was subjected to as an organizer, as well as the violations she witnessed against her co-workers:

Management is more repressive toward women; men earn one and a half times women's wages, they are given leave and wage rises if they demand them, but any woman who raises her voice faces the threat, too often carried into action, of dismissal. Women are so afraid of losing their jobs and face so many social obstacles that we often silence ourselves from protesting and tolerate extreme exploitation. If women lose their jobs, they face increased tension in their homes and may even be subjected to family violence, and this is another strong inhibiting factor to their organizing to realize their rights. Women who are struggling for their economic survival continue to face extreme repression and violence in society, in the workplace and in the home. Being women is our crime.

I want to share a personal experience with you.... Suddenly, one morning, a woman [worker] fell unconscious on the floor. The doctor could find nothing wrong with her. Later, when she regained consciousness, we heard the reason for her falling ill. Her husband was dead and she had a baby son. She had no source of financial support. Her house was almost three miles from the factory, and every day she had to walk all the way, work 12 hours, and then walk back again. On many occasions, she couldn't afford to eat all day, and had to spend whatever money she had to buy food and milk for her son. In the last six months, she had sold her blood on three occasions in order to buy milk for him. This is why she fainted.

We raised the issue with the management and tried to persuade them to raise her wages. They refused to listen to us, because we were only women workers. We were unorganized and we had no bargaining power....Men protest, but women face greater difficulties in protesting: social and cultural perceptions and restrictions on our mobility limit our employment possibilities.

Soon after this incident...when we were working inside, I suddenly felt suffocated, and in front of my eyes, 10 to 15 women slipped unconscious to the floor from their machines. I rushed to the gate, but found it locked. Several of us kept screaming for the gate to be opened, but no one came. We lay the unconscious women below the fan. I opened the windows and called for help and for the police. Some time later, the gate was opened. I kept shouting for people to call ambulances, or the women will die. We carried the women down and took them to the emergency ward. The doctor's report said they had been affected by some kind of gas. Management insisted we had fainted due to the heat. Our protest began....

The management began a policy of repression against all the workers and particularly targeted me. They used both the police and mastans (thugs) to harass us. Everyone in my [union] committee had their employment terminated. When we were told of the termination, the management's mastans were present. I left in fear of my life. After this, another nine workers were dismissed....I sought legal help, and after nine months the court gave judgement recognizing us as a trade union.

Finally, women suffer disproportionately under international economic restructuring. Structural Adjustment Programmes (SAPs) is the name given to economic policies imposed on so-called developing countries in order to promote free-market capitalism, secure debt repayment, and limit obstacles to the market such as minimum wage and benefits requirements, or mandatory environmental protection measures. The impact of SAPs is similar to that of polices being fostered in so-called advanced capitalist economies in the interest of economic competitiveness. In both cases, women are suffering the results. Elaine Hewitt from the Caribbean explained the gender-specific impact of SAPs in her region:

[M]any women in the Caribbean have the sole responsibility for the economic well being of their children. Over 40% of all households are female-headed. Given the low levels of wages and high levels of unemployment, the contribution of low-income women to family income is significant. Still in many countries of the Caribbean, there are no laws which grant women the right to maternity leave and pay. Women reproduce the society at their own economic risk.

In many countries, the lowest level of minimum wage is accorded to the household assistant. Indeed, in one country, the minimum wage for the household assistant is even less than the minimum wage for a juvenile. These workers are women. The undervaluing of this type of work, (cleaning, cooking, and child care) reflects most poignantly the societal perception of women's worth.

Women's economic vulnerability is deepened by the structural adjustment policies dictated by international financial institutions. In countries like Trinidad and Tobago, Jamaica, Guyana, and Barbados, resources are used to service the external debt at the expense of the social sector. Cutting government expenditure under Structural Adjustment Programmes has meant reduced access to health care, education, housing and social security benefits for women. The majority of those who have lost their jobs under these policies are also female, since women predominate in the social sector. In sum, this means greater poverty for women. The sector of the population which benefitted the least from the international loans (women and children) is now being made to bear the greatest burden....

Article 23 of the Universal Declaration, which calls for international cooperation for the realization of social and economic rights, has never been honoured. Women, bearers and rearers of children, carers of the aged and disabled, managers of households and producers of goods and services, feel most acutely the effects of the violations of these articles.

And there is a relationship between national economic underdevelopment and violence against women. While violence against women occurs within all classes, there is no disputing that the economic crisis reduces a woman's power to resist. Studies from Guyana, for example, suggest women of low-income status suffer violence more frequently. Women with few resources have less options.

I think of Tara's tragic story. Battered for 15 years by her husband, she finally found the courage to seek refuge in a shelter. Because she had to leave in emergency circumstances, Tara was forced to leave her children, two teenage sons and a daughter, behind. Tara has no resources of her own. She can't find accommodations to house her children and herself. There are no governmental support services to help her. She worked as a domestic employee, but lost her job because of her husband's threats to the employer. The children who had witnessed and hated the violence, now hate their mother for leaving them in order to save her own life.

Battered women are always forced to make difficult choices. These choices are the more tragic because women make them knowing that their quality of life may not improve.

I can attest to domestic violence. I am a survivor. I lived that life for more years than I care to remember. Why did I stay? I was a prisoner of the conspiracy of silence; I felt powerless. In believing that tomorrow could be better, I finally left, penniless, homeless, and with two children to support. It took me many years to recover. But I recovered despite the censure of society. What I have today is my self-esteem and my spiritual wellness. My sons only now understand the choice I had to make.

Judge's Statement: Justice P. N. Bhagwati

The testimony of these courageous women that we have just heard demonstrates the ways in which women are denied their basic economic and social rights, both within the home and in the workplace. These violations are in derogation of the human rights embodied in the *International Covenant on Economic, Social and Cultural Rights*, the Principle of Sexual Non-Discrimination found in the *United Nations Charter*, the *Universal Declaration of Human Rights*, and other international human rights instruments such as the *Convention on the Elimination of All Forms of Discrimination Against Women*.

There are various rights that are violated, which the testimony that has been given before us shows are denied to women. For example, indigenous women, migrant women, women engaged in domestic work, and so on. You have already heard the testimony, and I need not repeat all that has been said. But I wish to point out that social and economic structures are responsible for the denial of human rights to women as exemplified by the testimony before us. These socio-economic structures need to be changed so that women are recognized as independent, social and economic units entitled to their human rights, both within the family and outside. It is undoubtedly necessary to make laws, at the national, regional and international levels, but unless such laws are directed towards demolition of unjust social and economic structures—which are based on assumed male superiority, and which perpetuate discriminatory policies and practices against women and deny them their basic human rights—unless this is done, these laws will not be effective in bringing about change. So what is necessary is to direct our energies, not in taking individual cases on an ad hoc basis, but toward demolishing existing unjust socio-economic structures.

Of course, what is necessary is that women mobilize themselves for this task. Women can overcome violations of their human rights only if they unite and organize themselves. Men are not going to prevent violations of human rights of women. Their mind-set would not permit them to do so. Do not therefore depend upon men to help you. They have exercised domination and power over women for centuries. They are not easily going to give up that power. Power has to be wrested from unwilling hands. Women must therefore empower themselves. They must have a solidarity movement amongst them, uniting women from all parts of the world, in order to be able to fight for their rights. And if they do so, determinedly, with a sense of dedication and purpose—which we see here in ample measure—then men cannot resist for long. Let women raise a battle cry and freedom will be theirs.

Chapter 7
Political Persecution and Discrimination

Everyone has the right to take part in the government of his [her] country, directly or through freely chosen representatives. Everyone has the right to equal access to public service in his [her] country (art. 21).

UN UNIVERSAL DECLARATION OF HUMAN RIGHTS

Men and women of full age...are entitled to equal rights as to marriage, during marriage and at its dissolution. Marriage shall be entered into only with the free and full consent of the intending spouses (art 16).

UN UNIVERSAL DECLARATION OF HUMAN RIGHTS

....No one shall be subjected to arbitrary or unlawful interference with his [her] privacy (art. 17)....Everyone shall have the right to hold opinions without inter-ference. Everyone shall have the right of freedom of expression (art. 19).

UN INTERNATIONAL COVENANT ON CIVIL AND POLITICAL RIGHTS

The primary work of the international human rights community, particularly in the West, has been on defending civil and political rights. Yet, even within this area, many of the specific ways in which women are violated or denied these rights have remained invisible. The women testifying in this section sought to address this gap in human rights practice. They highlighted the gendered dimensions of civil and political rights, and demanded that these parameters be broadened so that the indivisibility of human rights for all prevails. Gender-based violations of the civil and political covenant have only recently begun to be addressed by groups like

Amnesty International which, for example, now documents rapes by agents of the government (such as police and the military) as forms of state-sponsored torture.

The testimonies in this section address three dimensions of political persecution and discrimination that women experience: several testifiers deal with different forms of gender-based persecution in detention as well as state-mediated harassment in civil society; these accounts demonstrate that with growing numbers of women migrants and refugees globally, a system of human rights protection based on one's membership in a nation-state is inadequate, especially where there is gender-blindness to the kinds of human rights violations that women in these situations face; and, in balancing the cultural and/or religious freedoms of groups against the rights of individuals, women's political and civil rights have all too often been sacrificed.

Demonstrating how gender is used in political persecution, Gertrude Fester, an anti-Apartheid activist, described the sexual humiliation which she and other women have been subjected to while in detention in South Africa:

It was just before 4:00 am and the house was surrounded by about 20 men, all armed. For the next 40 minutes, they walked around the house. Then at 4:30 the doorbell rang. Three enormous Afrikaner men dwarfed me....After they ransacked the house, they took me outside to the cars.

...I was asked to be a police spy for them. When I refused they became very aggressive and threatening. Various interrogators, about seven, stood around me. One played with his gun and laughed that it could 'accidentally' go off.

I was later informed that I was being detained under section 29...[and had] no rights: no access to lawyers or doctors of your own choice...; your friends and family are not informed where you are nor can they visit you; you can be detained...for six months and it can be renewed; you are not allowed any books, pens, paper, nothing. I was taken to the Wynberg police cells, where I was to be kept. There, for the first time, I saw a police woman....For section 29, you are watched 24 hours a day.

...That first night, as I opened the blankets to get into the bed, I was confronted with a drawing of an enormous erect penis on the sheet. I asked for another sheet but this was denied. I then made up the bed so that I could not see this penis nor touch it with any part of my body.

...In the offices where I was taken for interrogation, I was never let out of anyone's sight. I was therefore very puzzled that I had to be stripped when I returned from

interrogation. But I soon realized that it was to humiliate me rather than search me. It was this Captain's way of exercising his power over me. The Captain would stand at the door of my cell while shouting instructions to the two police women who were stripping me. After they took off my jacket, I decided to strip myself, throwing my clothes all around the cell. He would stand there bellowing orders. It was winter, but while I stood there naked, I never felt any cold, only humiliation, anger, and resentment at my powerlessness. Once they had left me, I would compose poems in my mind of these incidents.

....I was kept in solitary confinement for nearly four months. During this period, there were times when I was left in my cell for up to three weeks. No, they did not torture me during these periods; they knew that my mind was torturing me....[T]he fact that [my interrogator] was physically so much bigger and stronger than I was, that the state apparatus was on his side, my physical illness, hallucinations and insecurity about my sanity, the isolation, the fact that he was white and male really rendered me powerless sometimes. But then there were the other times when I confronted him and the illegitimacy of the state. When the correctness of what I stood for, and the inspiration of all those others who went before me and suffered far more than I was suffering, assisted me... .

[Later] while I was on trial, I was dismissed from the Department of Education and Culture on charges of misconduct. I know of many other male teachers employed by the same department who were never dismissed at all.

In February 1990, the African National Congress was legalized. So after one year and ten months, the charges were withdrawn. After my release, I had to spend three months in a hospital for nervous disorders. I want to emphasize that what happened to me was easy compared to what others have suffered.

Ana Rivera and Norma Valle, feminist activists from Puerto Rico, described a pattern of political persecution levied against women who organize to improve women's lives and who insist that women exercise their human right to equal participation in governmental decision-making and policy formulation. The political persecution of women activists in the areas of peace, social justice and female empowerment is not new, but it has rarely been given serious human rights attention. Ana Rivera's story follows:

[Below] is [an excerpt from a] memorandum which appears in dossier # 6288 of the Puerto Rican Police Intelligence Office. This dossier is mine. Due to my participa-

tion in a feminist organization and in activities to promote womens rights, the Puerto Rican police had tracked me and kept information about me under the category of subversive and terrorist:

November 25th, 1985

Memorandum to: Captain Carmelo Melendez, director of the Intelligence office. From: Agent Israel Santos.

Issue: Demonstration sponsored by the coordinator of feminist organization.

Reason for the activity: To celebrate the International Day Against Violence Against Women.

....Feminists have been organizing in Puerto Rico since the 1970s, in accordance with the rights that we have under the laws of the island. Under the constitution of the associate free state of Puerto Rico, the right to meet and freedom of association are guaranteed to the people. It is also guaranteed that we cannot be discriminated against for reasons of race, colour, origin, sex, and political and religious ideas. In 1972, we founded the Mujer Integrate Ahora; I was very young, only 16 years old, and I believed in justice. I did not know its consequences.

This practice of keeping files on individuals and persecuting people for their political ideas has a long history....This practice was questioned at a national tribunal, which demanded that the Puerto Rican Police and the Justice department stop the practice and return the dossiers to their respective owners. When we got our dossiers back, we realized that, according to the Puerto Rican government, it is subversive to believe in providing more opportunities for women in society.

....In the following decade, the surveillance was extended to members of other women's organizations too. For all the members of these organizations, this persecution had personal consequences that directly affected these women's lives. Some of them lost their jobs because officials would come to their work place to talk about them. Others had problems with their neighbours due to the police coming to interrogate them. And many times, the problems were with family and close friends. I, for example, suffered for many years because I did not know that they had invented a false case about me at the Puerto Rican University. It almost prevented me from continuing my law studies.

Norma Valle reports a similar experience:

....I've been a feminist activist since 1969. I was the president of the Sociedad de Mujeres Periodistas, la Federación de Mujeres Puertorriqueñas, and I was a member

of the board of directors of the Journalists' Union.

I have done all that under the harassment and the pressure of the state. I started to feel the discrimination just after I had been elected the president of the Federación de Mujeres Puertorriqueñas. I was persecuted and discriminated against during the nine years of work at the newspaper El Mundo. In 1975, I was transferred into five different departments of the editorial office in a period of five months. First, I was a political reporter, then I was transferred into the sports section, later I was a community reporter ('hot line'), and finally they changed my work hours. I felt a continuous pressure against me....

When, in 1989 the Supreme Tribunal of Puerto Rico ordered the release of more than 130,000 dossiers of persons who were considered subversives by the state, I received my dossier with information collected for more than a decade by the State police and the Justice department (file #5457). I was considered subversive for being a feminist. I found out that all the social pressure I suffered, the discrimination at work and my recurrent unemployment, were a result of consecutive visits by intelligence agents to my neighbors, my parents, and my bosses at the different jobs.... They had the plate number of my cars, they investigated all my private and confidential documents....they registered the people who had visited me. The harassment was real, concrete—I have the evidence in my hands.

María Olea, a Chilean immigrant to the United States, exposed the inadequacy of prevailing male-centred definitions of political persecution and citizenship, as well as the gender-based violations women immigrants to the North face:

As an immigrant woman I want to tell you how we are affected by the inhumane and racist laws that have been proposed in the US such as: that children born in the US to undocumented parents no longer be recognized as citizens of the country; that undocumented children not have the right to attend school; that pregnant women and their children not have access to health care, and if they seek assistance, the hospital must report them to immigration authorities.

The immigration laws in the United States also put women at a disadvantage. People immigrate for various reasons. Some flee political violence and war, others flee economic misery, others to reunite with families, and in some cases, as in my own, we run away from domestic violence. I escaped my country, Chile, in 1988 to save the lives of myself and my two children. I escaped a dictatorial political system that offered me absolutely no support as a battered woman; rather, the system sup-

ports men who are permitted to legally abuse their women. Because of this, I was forced to leave Chile, believing that the United States, a supposedly democratic country and a leader in the defense of human rights, would give me the protection I needed by granting me refugee status.

But, when I arrived in the country, I merely became another undocumented woman, because the legal system doesn't consider domestic violence against women as grounds for refugee protection. So in this way, my family and I became people without a country, because we could not return to our home without facing a risk to our lives, and in the United States, as 'illegals,' we were invisible. Many immigrant women are in the same painful situation. So that is why as a woman, as a mother, I ask the United Nations to support the recommendation that domestic violence be considered grounds for refugee status; in that way, we will save the lives of many women and children.

Khalida Messaoudi presented the case of "Oum Ali" (Mother of Ali), whose family has been persecuted by members of the fundamentalist Muslim community in which she resides because she was living without a man after her husband left her:

On June 5th, 1989 the local authority of the town received a petition, with 197 signatures, calling for their neighbourhood to be cleared of the presence of three women who were considered to have inappropriate lifestyles. They threatened these women. They mobilized groups of young boys to harass the women daily. When these 'undesirables' did not leave the community, a group of ten men decided to take action. On June 21, 1989 during the night, they came together, deliberated, and decided that fire was the only way to 'purify' the neighbourhood.

.... "Oum Ali" is a 34 year old woman, recently divorced, living alone with seven children. Abandoned by her husband before the divorce, illiterate, and without a job, she is the poorest of the poor, because under Islamic Law Family Code 52, neither she nor her children are protected—they do not receive any financial support.

....[The fundamentalists] accused her of prostitution, they accused her of making the neighbourhood impure, of affecting the morality, the religiousness of the Muslims, and the spiritual health of the town. Even if it was the case, even if she were a prostitute, they should know that if she went that route, it was because there were men willing to exploit her in the worst fashion that you can exploit another human being.....

During the night of the 22nd of June, at three in the morning, they began throw-

ing stones at the door of Oum Ali's modest home. Awakened by cries and the rain of the stones, she ran to her neighbour for assistance, but he slammed the door in her face. She then went to the police station, and on the way noticed a number of masked men were in her courtyard....At that moment, the aggressors were already over the wall and into her home. Her eldest daughter, 13 years old, brought the other children together, but had to leave behind her handicapped, 3 year old brother. The daughter ran back to the house to get him, but she saw the men coming in her direction and so only had time to hide the boy under the bed. The men came into the bedroom, one of them had a knife, another a can of heating oil which he threw over the bed and lit on fire in order to 'purify' the house.

The police did not come at first, until Oum Ali ran back and began screaming. This time they came, just as the corpse of her child, Ali, was being carried out. At six in the morning, the main instigator was arrested, and a few hours later, the twelve accomplices were arrested. Of the 13 criminals, 12 are married men with children of their own. None of the arsonists were unemployed. If men persecute and kill women, it is said that it is because of economic reasons; but this has nothing to do with economics, for she was not an economic threat to them. It has only to do with sexist ideology that found its expression this way.

The day the criminals were arrested, there was a big demonstration by the Islamic militants; they marched toward the police headquarters chanting and asking for the release of the arsonists. By their logic, they need not deny the crime. They believe they have the right to ensure that the religious precepts are properly followed by all....[T]hey have the right to persecute any person—particularly women who are alone, who they believe are representatives of Satan, representatives of danger and immorality—and the right to persecute any person who goes against their ideas actively or simply through their existence.

[T]he sentence was ridiculous considering the severity of the crime....The courts gave the heaviest sentence of 15 years to the principal instigator, 10 years to the next in charge, and less than 10 years each to the others.

Judge's Statement: The Honourable Gertrude Mongella

Dear brothers and sisters, it has been a hard day for us all. Before I give my judgement, maybe I should just pronounce a few words which have been repeated the whole day today: pain, traumatic, violence, terrorized, injustice, oppression, torture, misery, suffering, humiliation, anguish, cruelty, discrimination, sub-ordination, nervous disorder and occasionally punctuated by anger, despair, bitterness, and silence. I would like to say that the word "silence" is one we need to discuss at this World Conference on Human Rights. How long are the women of the world going to continue to be silent?

I would like to take this opportunity to thank all those who organized this Tribunal because it is a practical exposure of the long time silence of women, and as we prepare for the UN Fourth World Conference on Women (Beijing, 1995), I think this is the right footing.

May I now take an opportunity to thank all the women who have testified. I thank them for the courage, for the sacrifice they have once again made to play back the themes of their lives which kept us sniffing our noses and wiping our eyes.

Now, coming to political persecution and discrimination, it shows us one important thing, the absence of women in decision-making. We can trade all the paragraphs in the human rights documents, we can talk about women's rights being human rights, but as long as women remain absent from the decision-making bodies, it will take us a long time to make that idea successful.

The male judges understood what the women talked about. But sometimes, because they've never suffered any of these abuses which some of us have suffered in one way or another in a woman's life cycle—as a child, as a young woman, or as an elder—I think it was a very traumatic situation for them, and that's why they kept on saying, "Where are the other men?" So, for those who organized this conference or this meeting, can I ask them next time to balance the gender presence in our next audience if it ever happens.

What I have learned from the testimonies is their commonality which transcends the boundaries of nationality, race, culture, creed, ideology, time in history, educational background and class, and I can only say that we women are one. The testimonies have strengthened my conviction that, as we prepare for the Women's Conference in Beijing, the diversity among us should act as strength to come to a common goal and to act collectively. The testimonies of these brave women are genuine examples of structural and systematic persecution of women based on gender, race and class. Such persecution consistently occurs in pursuit of political and other vested interests. However, it uses all these other excuses—special laws, cultural and religious norms and traditions to provide a satisfying cover for the real causes of such persecution. And sometimes I wonder, why should women continue to go to churches and mosques, where we are told we are not equal to the other people? Why don't we look for our own god? A she god?

People are using religious covers, they're using culture, they're using the laws, and maybe it's because of women's ignorance of the law. We must tackle legal literacy to make sure that all women know what there is in all the laws of the faith and in the laws of the Koran and the Bible. I think we can argue from strength rather than weakness. We note with anguish that in the case of terrorism against women, the subordination of women goes beyond individual cases of violence to collective terrorist action. This is the challenge to the rule of the law, the principles of justice in the universality of human rights. We recognize the persecution of these women on account of their political activities, their gender, race or class, as violations of human rights contained in the *UN Universal Declaration of Human Rights*, in the *UN International Covenant on Civil and Political Rights*, in the *UN Convention on the Elimination of All Forms of Discrimination against Women*, in the *UN Declaration on the Elimination of All Forms of Intolerance and All Discrimination Based on Religion and Belief*. I want to congratulate these women who have provided testimony to this Tribunal for their extraordinary courage and perseverance.

I have come to the conclusion that if we had to look for a nation which has not violated any women's human rights, I doubt we could find one. So, if that's the case, why are we women so many times trapped into discussions and in debates of finger pointing, which distract us from addressing the issues. I want to announce here that I've been asked many times as the Secretary General of the World Conference on Women, why China? Why should we go to China? China violates human rights. Now, this morning, we've been hearing from North, South, West and East the violations of human rights. And I think I was correct, I kept on answering—show me any nation which has not violated women's human rights and we will have the Conference there.

Women here have talked with the same language, and I'm sure that if people heard without looking at them, we would not have been able to recognize where these women come from or what their colour is because of the similarities of the injustices inflicted on them. Why shouldn't we now, from today, create unity and move together to action, and leave out the petty issues which are used to divide us and distract us from the real discussions? I hope that when we meet in Beijing, when we are discussing the Platform for Action, we discuss it in the spirit of changing the world for a better world for women in the 21st century.

Chapter 8
Judges' Final Statement

t is with deep anguish and profound regret that we have heard the testimony today of 33 courageous women who have come from all parts of the world. Their accounts show that the nature and extent of violations of women's human rights continue to be cruel and pervasive. These violations remain not only unremedied but also unrecognized as discriminatory or as an affront to women's human dignity. This widespread failure to recognize, honour and protect women's human rights poses a challenge to the credibility, universality, and justice of international human rights law.

We affirm the principle of universality which affords protection to all of humanity, including women. (Universal human rights standards are rooted in all cultures, religions and traditions.) We need to learn from all cultures, religions and traditions to deepen our understanding of human rights for women. However, while recognizing cultural pluralism, those cultural, religious and traditional practices that derogate from universally accepted human rights and prove harmful to women cannot be tolerated.

We note with dismay that international human rights law has not been applied effectively to redress the disadvantages and injustices experienced by women solely because of their gender. In this sense, respect for human rights fails to be universal. The testimony shows that the reasons for this general failure include:

▶ a lack of understanding of the systemic nature of the subordination of women and social, political and economic structures which perpetuate such subordination;

▶ the failure to recognize the subordination of women, particularly in the private sphere, as violations of their human rights;

▶ an appalling failure or neglect by the state to condemn and provide redress for discrimination and other violations of women's human rights;

▶ we call upon this World Conference on Human Rights to recognize and condemn violations of women's human rights as violations of everyone's rights in every corner of the world.

Also, we call upon this World Conference on Human Rights, the United Nations, and Member States to establish mechanisms to prevent, investigate, and to provide redress for violations of women's rights and to this end we recommend:

1. The establishment of an International Criminal Court for Women to protect and enforce women's human rights including sexual abuse, mass rape and forced pregnancy in armed conflict;

2. The strengthening and enforcement of the *Convention on the Elimination of All Forms of Discrimination Against Women*, by urging:

   ▶ universal ratification of this Convention;

   ▶ withdrawal of all reservations to the Convention which perpetuate women's subordination, where made upon ratification;

   ▶ effective implementation and the elimination of cultural, religious and traditional stereotypes and practices which impede such implementation. This should include the re-interpretation of religious norms in light of the principles of human rights;

   ▶ development of a mechanism for women who have been denied access to justice within their own countries to bring their complaints, under an Optional Protocol, before the Committee on the Elimination of Discrimination against Women (CEDAW);

3. The integration of gender perspectives in all human rights committees established under human rights treaties to ensure the application of all human rights treaties to all forms of subordination of women;

4. The expansion of the work of the UN and its specialized agencies for preventing and redressing all forms of violations of women's rights. We recognize that these cruel and pervasive violations of women's rights retard the progress and development of society and can be prevented by treating women fairly and justly;

5. The need to recognize that many of these violations take place in the private sphere of the family and that domestic violence is a violation of human rights.

We recommend that the 1994 UN Year of the Family recognize all forms of supportive relationships that exist inside and outside institutionalized family arrangements;

6. The adoption by the General Assembly of the United Nations of the *Draft Declaration on the Prohibition of Violence Against Women;* and

7. The establishment of a Special Rapporteur with a broad mandate to investigate violations of women's human rights.

We call upon the non-governmental organizations, in conjunction with the media, to continue and expand their investigation and reporting of violations of women's human rights, and to empower women through training to expose denials of justice for women by all organs of state and by individuals.

We would like to close by underscoring the cruel and pervasive nature of the violations inflicted upon you. We congratulate you for your courage in giving your testimony and for your determination to give visibility to these violations and abuses to which you and many other women around the world are continuously exposed.

Your courage will inspire other women to speak out and to demand their human rights, and will encourage others to work for the vindication of these violations.

The voices of these women have broken the silence. Their appeal to the world must be heard, recognized, investigated, sanctioned and redressed.

Panel on Human Rights Abuse in the Family

The testimony by these seven brave women expose violations that take place within the private sphere of the family. In profound ways, the testimony challenges :

▶ idealistic views of the family and the perception of women within the family;

▶ the notion that human rights abuses don't occur in the private sphere; and,

▶ the argument that women do not need protection for the abuses that take place within the family.

Our reaction to the testimony is that women have been subjected to severe pain and suffering, whether physical or mental, intentionally inflicted on these women for the purposes of punishing or intimidating or coercing women.

This constitutes torture according to the *International Convention against Torture and Other Cruel, Inhumane or Degrading Treatment or Punishment.* Because these violations take place within the private sphere of the family, they are not characterized as torture.

The testimony also shows that women's rights to private and family life protected by human rights treaties have been violated in profound ways, and that states have not provided women with any effective means of redress.

Panel on War Crimes Against Women

These testimonies bring to light gross violations of the human rights of women that have heretofore been ignored by the human rights community. When they occur in war and situations of armed conflict, they constitute grave breaches of the *Fourth Geneva Convention Relative to the Protection of Civilian Persons in Time of War* and customary international humanitarian law. In particular, we underscore that rape, forced prostitution and forced pregnancy constitute torture.

Where these violations are systematic and widespread, they amount to crimes against humanity both because of the severity of the violence and because they are persecutions based on gender. In other words, these women are being subjected to particular, sex-specific forms of violence because they are women. Rapes committed on a mass scale as a tool of "ethnic cleansing" also represent crimes against humanity.

The testimonies also demonstrate the ways that violations of women's human rights are exacerbated by war, and illustrate the connections between public, and in this case military violence, and private violence.

Where this violence is permitted to continue unremedied by the state, it constitutes gross violations of human rights and crimes against humanity. Those responsible for these acts, especially for grave breaches of the *Geneva Conventions*, must be brought to justice. Legal accountability is essential for women's recovery and the rehabilitation of their communities.

Panel on Violations of Bodily Integrity

The testimony of these five remarkable women shows that violations of bodily integrity are brutal, systematic and structural. These atrocities are an affront to their human dignity. They are often justified by reference to cultural norms and misinterpretations of religious and other traditions. They violate women's rights to:

- liberty and security of the person
- private and family life
- freedom from torture and other cruel, inhuman or degrading treatment or punishment
- freedom from all forms of discrimination
- health and appropriate health care services

The testimony addressing trafficking in women, rape of disabled women, genital mutilation, persecution of women because of their sexual orientation, and denial of women's rights to health, including reproductive health care services and information, provides evidence of grave violations of women's human rights under many national constitutions and international and regional human rights conventions including:

- the *UN Universal Declaration of Human Rights* (Articles 3, 5, and 12),
- the *UN International Covenant of Civil and Political Rights* (Articles 7, 9.1, and 17),
- the *UN Convention Against Torture and Other Cruel, Inhumane or Degrading Treatment or Punishment* (Article 2),
- the *UN Convention on the Elimination of All Forms of Discrimination Against Women* (Articles 5.a, 6, 10.h and 12),
- the *African Charter on Human and Peoples Rights* (Articles 5 and 16).

We recognize these abuses of the bodily integrity and dignity of women as violations of women's rights. They should be addressed and remedied at the national, regional and international levels. Moreover, every effort by governments, the United Nations and specialized agencies has to be made immediately to address:

- the prevention of such abuses through the implementation of human rights instruments, and education and training in order to empower women to use these instruments for vindication of their rights;

 ▶ the elimination of the root causes of such violations which attempt to justify themselves on the basis of cultural and other traditions including stereotypes which assign inferior and degrading roles to women to the detriment of their dignity and health.

Panel on Socio-Economic Rights

The testimony of these women demonstrates the ways in which women are denied their basic economic and social rights both within the home and in the workplace. These violations are in derogation of the human rights found in the *International Covenant on Economic, Social and Cultural Rights* and the principles of sexual non-discrimination found in the *United Nations Charter*, the *Universal Declaration of Human Rights* and, for example, the *Convention on the Elimination of All Forms of Discrimination Against Women*. These include:

 ▶ the right to life
 ▶ the right to freedom of association
 ▶ the right to equal remuneration and benefits, including equal treatment as to work of equal value
 ▶ the right to social services, food and child care
 ▶ the right to occupational health and safety
 ▶ the right of rural women to have their particular problems recognized
 ▶ the right to temporary special measures for women to achieve equality
 ▶ the right to education
 ▶ the right of women to be free from stereotyping on account of their gender

Each testimony exemplifies the universal devaluation of women's work that renders them economically dependent and increases their vulnerability. In particular, women are unable to leave violent situations in the home as a result of their economic dependence, nor can they leave their jobs when sexually harassed or abused in the work place out of fear that they will lose their jobs and be rendered destitute. Women who have attempted to assert their economic and social rights or to organize around such rights have been exposed to extreme violence in the home or threatened with loss of employment and economic opportunity.

The testimony also demonstrated how women live in very diverse economic and social units and arrangements, such as:

▶ single women and mothers

▶ prostituted women living with their children, and

▶ mothers living in non-marital relationships

As long as these diverse arrangements remain unrecognized or invisible, women, especially single women, will continue to bear the major burden of the sexually discriminatory economic policies of states. In this respect, The Tribunal expresses its concern about the 1994 UN Year of the Family in so far as it promotes a particular form of the family. The testimony exemplifies how the traditional family is:

▶ built on unequal power relationships and is oppressive to women;

▶ denies the existence of women who do not live within this traditional unit; and

▶ compromises other economic and social arrangements and understanding of family.

Panel on Political Persecution and Discrimination

The testimonies of these brave women are genuine examples of structural and systematic persecution of women based on their gender, race and class. Such persecution consistently occurs in pursuit of political and other vested interests. However, it uses or rather abuses, special laws, cultural and religious norms and traditions to provide a justifying cover for the real causes of such persecution. In the majority of the cases of political persecution of women, whether by state authorities, terrorists or fundamentalist groups, they are based on deep-rooted biases which subordinate women.

We note with anguish that in the case of terrorism against women, the subordination of women goes beyond individual cases of violence to collective terrorist action. This is a defiant challenge to the rule of law, the principles of justice and the universality of human rights.

We recognize the persecution of these women on account of their political activities, their gender, race or class as violations of human rights under:

▸ the *Universal Declaration of Human Rights,*

▸ the *International Covenant on Civil and Political Rights,*

▸ the *Convention on the Elimination of All Forms of Discrimination Against Women,* and

▸ the *Declaration on the Elimination of All Forms of Intolerance and of Discrimination based on Religion or Belief.*

We congratulate these women who have provided testimony to this Tribunal for their extraordinary courage and perseverance. We call upon the World Conference to recognize and condemn these violations of women's human rights as violations of everyone's rights in every corner of the world.

Part III
Vienna Successes and Future Challenges

In addition to conducting The Tribunal, the Global Campaign for Women's Human Rights was active on many levels at the World Conference on Human Rights. This section describes many of the strategies of the Global Campaign in Vienna, both within the NGO area and at the United Nations Conference. It analyzes the Vienna Declaration *and the commitments to female human rights that were obtained through women's organizing around the Vienna conference. Finally, it concludes with a discussion of the challenges that lie ahead in seeking to implement women's human rights demands beyond Vienna.*

Chapter 9
NGO Activity and the
Media in Vienna

There were many women's activities and strategies at the World Conference on Human Rights that added to the impact of women's presence there, not all of which were part of the Global Campaign. One of the greatest successes of women's organizing was that almost half of the NGO participants present were women—an unprecedented number for a UN World Conference that was not focused specifically upon women or children. (Unfortunately, these percentages did not hold true for the government delegations to the World Conference which reflected the gender imbalance in governments around the world.)

The NGO initiatives discussed below are primarily ones in which the Center for Women's Global Leadership participated or had some direct involvement. In addition, a wide range of women's groups and human rights NGOs organized dozens of panels, workshops and events which addressed violations of women's human rights and supported women's organizing during the Vienna Conference. In the NGO fringe activity area, there were organized forums and activities that focused on themes ranging from war crimes against women and women's civil and political rights, to female sexual slavery and trafficking, women's reproductive and health rights, as well as socio-economic rights. Over the weekend of June 19-20, when the official conference center was closed, an NGO Tent City on Donau Island included many women's workshops organized primarily by local women's groups in Vienna. There were also several dramatic women's demonstrations at the entrance to the Conference, particularly around the issue of rape and war, which included a Women in Black vigil and women lying down in front of the doors in protest over war crimes against women in Bosnia.

It is impossible to name all the groups involved in these various projects, but in addition to those mentioned later in this chapter, activities were organized by groups such as Asia Pacific Forum on Women, Law and Development; Asian Women's Human Rights Council; Change, Inc; Church Women United; CLADEM (Latin American Committee for Women's Rights); Coalition for Immigrant and Refugee Rights; Columbia University's Development Law and Policy Programme; Coordinadora Mexicana de Defensoras Populares; Development Alternatives with Women for a New Era (DAWN); Foundation Against Sex Trafficking; Human Rights Watch Women's Project; Institute for Women Law and Development; International Lesbian and Gay Association; International Council of Women; International Women's Human Rights Law Clinic at the City University of New York; International Women's Rights Action Watch; ISIS International; Latin American and Caribbean Women's Health Network; Madre; Purple Roof Foundation; Refugee Women in Development (RefWID); Sisterhood is Global; Terra Femina; Terre des Femmes; Third World Movement Against the Exploitation of Women (TWMAEW); Women Against Fundamentalism; Women in Black; Women in Law and Development Africa; Women's International League for Peace and Freedom; Women Living Under Muslim Laws International Solidarity Network; and others.

The Rights Place for Women

"The Rights Place for Women," conceived and co-sponsored by the Austrian Coalition for Women's Human Rights, the Center for Women's Global Leadership, and the International Women's Tribune Centre, gave women a concrete gathering and information point and also provided visibility for women's organizing during the Conference. The Rights Place consisted of a large double room—one part of which was used for office work and the other for small meetings and information dissemination—and a portion of the corridor outside the room, which was set up with displays of women's literature, posters on the walls, and small tables and chairs for informal gatherings. The Rights Place was located in a central spot on the lower floor of the Austria Centre, where the NGOs were based, and thus it was almost impossible for anyone moving around in the NGO space to miss seeing that women were there in large numbers. It was also adjacent to the Women's Press Room organized by the Communications Consortium and close to the NGO organizing committee offices.

The Rights Place served as a space to which people could come at any time to find out what was happening with and about women, both in the NGO area and at the UN World Conference which was held upstairs in the Austria Centre. Women used it to convene meetings, exchange information, plan logistics pertaining to NGO events, and strategize on steps to advance women's human rights. Women gathered informally throughout the day to discuss major conference issues as they arose and to call sessions to discuss what actions to take. The room was equipped with telephones and computers for the use of those organizing women's events or engaged in drafting documents and statements related to the integration of women into working groups, panels, caucuses, or plenary interventions.

The Rights Place was also the main venue for organizing and implementing the logistics related to The Global Tribunal, including the provision of orientation and assistance to the 33 speakers and their support persons in the days preceding and following The Tribunal. The women who worked and volunteered in The Rights Place, who were primarily from the sponsoring organizations, also endeavoured to answer voluminous requests for logistical information and to give a general orientation to the Conference. The Austrian Women's Human Rights Coalition also compiled and distributed an extensive *Women's Guide*, which covered Conference events addressing women's human rights, as well as places and activities of interest to women in Vienna itself. Over all, The Rights Place established a visible sense of women's organized presence and their determination to be a recognized part of the human rights scene.

Media Strategies

Women's networks and media played a crucial role throughout the Global Campaign for Women's Human Rights by disseminating the petition and call for hearings, and letting women know about activities related to the UN World Conference. Many of the women's media groups were present in Vienna and continued to serve this function. They were aided by the International Women's Tribune Centre and ISIS International Chile, both of whom had spread word of the campaign through their networks and in their periodicals before the Conference, and then helped to coordinate the display of women's materials, including posters and publications, in and around The Rights Place in Vienna. In addition, both before and during the Vienna Conference, Global Campaign information was available through e-mail, via PeaceNet, and women were given training by members of several organizations, including the Association for Progresive Communications and the Foundation for a Compassionate Society, on how to use computer networking as a communications tool.

Feminist International Radio Endeavor (FIRE) also played a critical role by broadcasting information about the Global Campaign for Women's Human Rights and encouraging women to get involved in the processes pertaining to the World Conference on Human Rights. In Vienna, they conducted interviews with women active in promoting human rights, and coordinated a Radio Tribunal each afternoon in The Rights Place. The Global Tribunal had been planned in the months preceding Vienna—through a regional process of selecting speakers with an International Coordinating Committee—and it was not possible to add testimony from women who arrived in Vienna eager to speak. The Radio Tribunal, on the other hand, was available for any woman, and it recorded interviews with those who wanted to present their cases in a public venue to raise awareness and contribute to the documentation of female human rights abuse. The interviews were broadcast on shortwave radio on a number of occasions, and are a rich source of information about women's human rights.

While the women's alternative media internationally is enormously important in linking women and in appraising parts of the wider public of women's concerns, the Global Campaign also sought to reach the mainstream media in order to establish a broader understanding of women's rights as human rights. In particular, the organizers decided that The Tribunal would be an event aimed at attracting media attention. However, there are obstacles to getting the "right" kind of media for women's concerns, and women have had varying degrees of success in gaining constructive, non-sensational and non-sexist visibility in mainstream media at local and national levels. Gaining access to the increasingly influential global media, such as Cable News Network (CNN), without losing control of the message, is an even greater challenge.

Recognizing these concerns, the Communications Consortium, which has considerable experience positioning women's perspectives in mainstream United States media, set up a women's press room in Vienna as a resource to women who wanted to gain coverage in the US and global mainstream media. In collaboration with key groups in the Campaign, the Consortium held information briefings and issued press releases on behalf of the Global Campaign. They solicited and edited thematic articles by diverse women on female human rights concerns, facilitated interviews by print and television journalists with Campaign leaders, and worked to promote The Tribunal and its demands as well as to bring attention to the individual cases presented. In addition, the Consortium endeavoured to support women journalists in Vienna who were working to influence their local or national media. The Consortium played a major role in securing press coverage of women's concerns in places like *The Washington Post* and *The New York Times*, as well as in a 10 minute slot featuring The Tribunal on CNN. During and immediately after Vienna, some of these articles and interviews were picked up by wire services and thus reached a broader readership internationally.

Prior to going to Vienna, the Center worked with Augusta Productions to pull together an international video team with members from Canada, Brazil and Austria. This group of individuals filmed The Tribunal, conducted interviews with women who had played instrumental roles in the Global Campaign for Women's Human Rights, and obtained footage of women's activities in The Rights Place and other locations, including the UN World Conference proceedings. The result is a 48-minute video account of women making their presence felt at the Vienna Conference, with a focus on The Tribunal. Women's Feature Service, based in New Delhi, India, also produced a one half hour video on The Tribunal, as well as several feature stories. National Public Radio and Pacifica Radio in the US, the United Nations Radio, and FIRE produced programmes based on The Tribunal, and audio tapes of it are available in both Spanish and English. (*See Part IV, Document H* for a list of videos, tapes, publications and other media-related outcomes of Vienna.)

While this media activity took time and occasionally overwhelmed the participants in the events, it also succeeded in getting the message of the Global Campaign for Women's Human Rights out beyond those people and groups present in Vienna. As a consequence of the extensive media coverage of women in Vienna, and of women's activities around human rights at the local level over the past four years, a noticeable increase in the understanding of women's rights as human rights is occurring. This can be seen, for example, in the increasing use of the language of human rights—torture, slavery, freedom of expression, right to assembly, etc.—in discussing obstacles to the achievement of women's rights. The adoption of such language enhances the possibility of utilizing human rights instruments and resources to achieve full human rights for women.

Chapter 10
Women's Lobbying and the Vienna Declaration

The United Nations World Conference on Human Rights was organized with a mandate from the UN General Assembly to review and appraise the status of human rights in the world today and to recommend better mechanisms to achieve universal human rights. Like most UN World Conferences, it was to produce a document reflecting governmental consensus on how to achieve these objectives. Even though women had succeeded in getting many of their concerns into the draft agenda at the final international Preparatory Committee meeting for the UN World Conference, they could not be certain that this text would remain in the Conference document throughout the Conference proceedings in Vienna unless the pressure to address women's human rights continued.[1] Many women also hoped to achieve a more extensive coverage of women's concerns than was contained in the draft agenda, and were therefore very active in a variety of lobbying efforts in their own countries prior to the Conference as well as in Vienna.

One of the early opportunities for women to show their strength in Vienna was the NGO Forum. It was a three day meeting of about 2000 people who aimed to influence the outcome of the official proceedings by preparing a unified NGO doc-

---

[1] Generally at UN World Conferences, most of the text of the final document is developed beforehand in the various regional and international preparatory meetings. What is discussed at the actual conference is primarily those items that are not yet agreed upon and thus have been put in "brackets." This can confuse those who expect a full discussion of all matters relevant to the topic because areas already agreed upon are not usually negotiated there. Further, it often disappoints those not involved in the preparatory processes who come hoping to introduce new ideas at the World Conference.

ument addressed to the Conference. The Forum was organized into five working groups that were to prepare text in the following areas:

▶ to review and evaluate the overall effectiveness of human rights mechanisms, and to identify obstacles and means to overcome them;

▶ to assess the protection of minorities and indigenous people's rights;

▶ to assess the protection of women's human rights;

▶ to examine the relation between human rights, democracy and development;

▶ to examine contemporary trends in human rights violations, including those related to racism, xenophobia, ethnic violence, and religious intolerance.

The women who had been active in the Global Campaign during the preparatory process towards Vienna made a strategic decision to distribute themselves throughout all five of the working groups. This way, the gender dimensions of each group's mandate would be addressed and the working group on women would not be the only location where women's concerns were heard. The Boltzmann Institute chose a chair, a rapporteur, and a resource person to prepare the background paper for each of the five working groups. Influenced by the women's campaign, they chose at least one woman for these jobs in each of the five working groups.

For the working group on women's human rights, Boltzmann asked Asma Jahangir of Pakistan to be the chair, Florence Butegwa of Uganda to be the rapporteur, and Charlotte Bunch of the US to prepare the background paper. The background paper gave a brief introduction to women's human rights perspectives, and then presented the Women's Caucus paper from the final international Preparatory Committee meeting. For a day and a half, over 200 women and a handful of men—most of them new to the Global Campaign for Women's Human Rights—discussed and revised the Women's Caucus statement presented in the background paper. Eventually, the NGO working group on women affirmed and expanded on the demands women had made up to Vienna, and worked to strengthen and elaborate those claims. When Florence Butegwa delivered the final version of the working group's statement to the NGO Forum Plenary, it was greeted with a standing ovation, sending a strong message to the UN World Conference that women were a constituency to be taken seriously.

Equally important, the statements from each of the other working groups included substantial references to women and gender perspectives on other aspects of human rights. All the working groups were asked to produce a short version of their demands, which were then pulled together and sent to the UN World Conference as the NGOs' common position. The working group on women also developed an extended version of their paper which outlines further areas of work needed to advance women's human rights beyond what is included in the *Vienna Declaration.* (See *Part IV, Document E* for the full statement prepared by the NGO working group on women.)

Throughout the Conference following the NGO Forum, a Women's NGO Caucus convened downstairs at the Austria Centre on a regular basis in order to assess the Conference proceedings and their implications for women. Many of the participants in the Caucus utilized the demands of the women's working group statement to develop lobbying initiatives around specific items in the official Conference document. A lobby group from the Caucus met daily to keep track of the drafting process in the government Conference and to ensure that the gains that had been made in Geneva were not lost. They responded to threats of new clauses inimical to women's human rights in addition to drafting new text for delegates to introduce.

The Caucus also debated substantive issues raised by the women's working group statement and by women who wanted more out of the *Vienna Declaration.* A tension existed between the fuller human rights demands that women wanted addressed and the gains that were actually possible at this particular conference. Those who had been involved in the process prior to Vienna tended to feel that the proposed text represented substantial progress for women, while many new to the process felt that the draft declaration was much too limited in its commitment to women. All these positions and activities enriched the debates around securing women's human rights and they also, helped to expand and develop women's leadership for the future.

Another major initiative in Vienna was a daily women's caucus organized by UNIFEM (United Nations Development Fund for Women), which was held upstairs at the Austria Centre where the governments were meeting. This caucus brought together women governmental delegates and women from the NGO Women's Caucus and from UN agencies to explore possible means to collaborate to advance women's human rights at the Conference in Vienna as well as afterwards. These sessions not only addressed the *Vienna Declaration,* but also went beyond it to look at how to integrate gender perspectives and women's human rights into the regular operations of the United Nations. At the UNIFEM-sponsored women's caucus, meetings were held with staff from the UN Centre for Human Rights, with members of the monitoring committees for various Treaty Bodies, and with some of the thematic and country rapporteurs in order to examine how gender consciousness would affect work in their areas.

Meanwhile, at the plenary sessions of the UN World Conference, women sought to make their voices heard in various ways. The NGO Women's Caucus gained time slots for six short presentations from its members, and a number of international NGOs spoke about the human rights of women. As a result of women's lobbying, several government delegates also included references to women in their official presentations, as did some of the United Nations agencies personnel. In this way, women's concerns were coming from all sectors, and it became increasingly difficult for any country to say that they were against women being included in the final declaration.

Women also negotiated with the Conference Secretariat to secure time on the agenda for a report on The Tribunal so that its recommendations would be officially recorded as part of the documentation of the World Conference on Human Rights. These negotiations included arranging with the secretariat and security officials for delivery of the third round of 270,000 petition signatures to the Conference floor immediately before the report on The Tribunal was made. On June 17, 1993, tens of thousands of signed petitions demanding human rights for women were delivered to the podium of the plenary hall, bringing the total of signatures received by the UN to almost half a million. Meanwhile, as the delegates looked up to see what was going on, Florence Butegwa and Charlotte Bunch stood up in the back of the hall where NGOs were allowed to speak and presented a statement on behalf of The Tribunal. The statement endorsed many of the demands made by the women's NGOs, and added a call from The Tribunal judges for the "establishment of an International Criminal Court for Women to protect and enforce women's human rights." It concluded with a warning to governments to recognize that the demands women were making at the Conference were not "an appeal on behalf of a special interest group, but rather, a demand to restore the birthright of half of humanity" (see *Part IV, Document D*).

The presentation from The Tribunal was followed by three speakers from the NGO Women's Caucus. Mary Kazunga of Zambia interrupted the business-as-usual noisiness in the room by calling for a minute of silence. With her stop watch held high in the air, she brought the delegates to a standstill and then asked them to remember all the women around the world who had died or been badly injured by domestic violence during that minute. Women had arrived on the Conference agenda.

Commitments of the Vienna Conference to Women's Human Rights

The *Vienna Declaration and Programme of Action* was adopted by the consensus of 171 member states of the United Nations at the close of the World Conference on Human Rights in Vienna on June 26, 1993 (see *Part IV, Document F*). It is the most recent and authoritative statement of the international community's commitment to human rights as a framework for the 21st century in global relations, social interaction, and the rights of individuals. Women should know what commitments their governments have made regarding the elimination of violations of women's human rights. This document can be used for political and moral leverage in calling on local and national authorities to live up to the international standards to which they have agreed. The *Vienna Declaration* also affirms other United Nations human rights instruments, such as the *Convention on the Elimination of All Forms of Discrimination Against Women* (CEDAW) and the Declaration on the Elimination of Violence Against Women.

The impact women had on the outcome of the Conference is first evident in the preamble to the *Vienna Declaration*, which states that the World Conference on Human Rights is "deeply concerned by various forms of discrimination and violence to which women continue to be exposed all over the world." It goes on to state that "the human rights of women and of the girl-child are an inalienable, integral and indivisible part of universal human rights." Further, "[t]he human rights of women should form an integral part of the United Nations human rights activities, including the promotion of all human rights instruments relating to women" (Part I, paragraph 18).

Another major theme of the document important for women is the reaffirmation of the universality of human rights regardless of differences in political, economic and cultural systems. This was a major battle throughout the Conference proceedings, and is especially crucial for women whose human rights are often eclipsed in the name of protecting diverse cultures or traditions. In addition, the *Vienna Declaration* reiterated that all human rights are "indivisible, ...interdependent and interrelated," which is to say that one set of rights, for example political and civil, is not more important than another, such as economic, social, or cultural.

The human rights of women were singled out for attention in a number of sections throughout the *Vienna Declaration* in addition to the section specifically addressing women's human rights. For example, with regard to the human rights of children, the *Vienna Declaration* urges "States to repeal existing laws and regulations and remove customs and practices which discriminate against and cause harm to the girl-child." It further calls for effective measures against female infanticide and other violations affecting girls, such as "harmful child labour, sale of children and organs, child prostitution, child pornography, as well as other forms of sexual abuse" (Part II, paragraphs 48 & 49). The Conference statement expressed deep concern about "violations of human rights during armed conflict, affecting the civilian population, especially women..." and called upon "States and all parties to strictly observe humanitarian law" in this regard (Part I, paragraph 29). In addition, the *Vienna Declaration* included discrimination against women in its condemnation of "gross and systematic violations" that "constitute serious obstacles to the full enjoyment of all human rights" (Part I, paragraph 30).

There are nine paragraphs under the title "The equal status and human rights of women" in Part II of the *Vienna Declaration and Programme of Action*. The critical points of this section include a recognition of the importance of "working toward the elimination of violence against women in public and private life" as well as "the elimination of all forms of sexual harassment, exploitation and trafficking in women." The section also calls for "the elimination of gender bias in the administration of justice and the eradication of any conflicts which may arise between the rights of women and the harmful effects of certain traditional or customary practices, cultural prejudices and religious extremism." Regarding conflict and war situations, the document affirms that violations of women's human rights, including "murder, systematic rape, sexual slavery, and forced pregnancy," are violations of the fundamental principles of international human rights and humanitarian law (paragraph 38).

Concerning health and reproductive rights, the *Vienna Declaration* states that women ought to enjoy the "highest standard of physical and mental health throughout their life span" and have access to "adequate health care and the widest range of family planning services" (paragraph 41). This section also "underlines the importance of the integration and full participation of women as both agents and beneficiaries in the development process" (paragraph 36). It further asserts that the "human rights of women should be integrated into the mainstream of United Nations system-wide activity" (paragraph 37).

Specific human rights policy recommendations include urging that: treaty monitoring bodies, special rapporteurs, and working groups facilitate women's access to these avenues of redress and "include the status of women in their deliberations and findings" (paragraph 42); the Commission on the Status of Women and the Committee on the Elimination of All Forms of Discrimination Against Women should "quickly examine" the possibility of introducing an individual complaints procedure to *CEDAW* (paragraph 40); as well as the universal ratification and/or a reduction in the excessive number of reservations to that convention (paragraph 39). The Conference also supported the decision of the Commission on Human Rights to consider appointing a special rapporteur on violence against women at its 1994 session, called upon the General Assembly to adopt the *Draft Declaration on Violence Against Women,* and urged States to "combat violence against women according to its provisions" (paragraph 38).

UN Declaration and Special Rapporteur on Violence Against Women

The process of developing a *UN Declaration on the Elimination of Violence against Women* was already in motion before Vienna, but it received an extra impetus from the women's campaign around the World Conference. The idea of this *Declaration* was initiated by an expert group of the UN Commission on the Status of Women in 1991 which sought to address the lack of any specific mention of violence against women in other UN treaties, including the *UN Convention on the Elimination of All Forms of Discrimination against Women.* The text for a *Declaration* was discussed and developed over the next year, and enjoyed an unusually rapid adoption by the General Assembly in December 1993. The *Declaration on the Elimination of Violence against Women* provides, for the first time, a definition of violence against women to which all of the member states of the United Nations have agreed. It states that violence against women is "any act of gender-based violence that results in, or is likely to result in, physical, sexual or psychological harm or suffering to women, including threats of such acts, coercion or arbitrary deprivations of liberty, whether occurring in public or private life" (art. 1). The definition continues to specify violence in the family as including battery, sexual abuse of female children, marital rape, dowry-related violence and female genital mutilation. It also cites violence in the general community including rape, sexual abuse, and sexual harassment at places of work, in educational institutions and elsewhere. Finally, the definition includes violence perpetrated or condoned by the state, wherever it occurs.

The *Declaration* also stipulates that the responsibilities of states to eliminate such violence at the national level are a matter of human rights policy; states should ensure that women who are subjected to violence have "access to the mechanisms of justice and...to just and effective remedies for the harm that they have suffered; States should also inform women of their rights in seeking redress through such remedies" (art. 4 (d)). States should develop "preventative approaches [to gender-based violence]...and ensure that the re-victimization of women does not occur because of laws insensitive to gender considerations" (art. 4(f)). Governments are also to provide "adequate resources for their activities related to the elimination of violence against women" (art. 4 (h)). In addition, States are called upon to "facilitate and enhance the work of the women's movement...in raising awareness and alleviating the problem of violence against women" (art. 4 (o)).

At the international level, States are called upon to ratify *CEDAW* and withdraw any reservations they hold to the convention (art. 4(a)). Also, in the course of "submitting reports as required under relevant human rights instruments of the United Nations, information pertaining to violence against women and measures taken to implement the present Declaration" should be included (art. 4 (m)).

In March 1994, the 50th session of the Commission on Human Rights responded to the *Vienna Declaration* with the adoption of a resolution on Integrating the Rights of Women into the Human Rights Mechanisms of the United Nations. This resolution featured the appointment for a three-year period of "a special rapporteur on violence against women, including its causes and consequences, who will report to the Commission on an annual basis" beginning in 1995 (paragraph 6). Radhika Coomaraswamy, a lawyer from Sri Lanka, was subsequently appointed to be the special rapporteur. Her mandate is outlined in paragraph 7 of the resolution and will be carried out "within the framework of the *Universal Declaration of Human Rights* and all international human rights instruments," including *CEDAW*. She has the responsibility to "seek and receive information on violence against women" and its "causes and consequences," and to "respond effectively" to that information. The special rapporteur may request such input from governments, treaty bodies, United Nations specialized agencies, other special rapporteurs, intergovernmental and non-governmental organizations, including women's organizations. She is also supposed to "recommend measures, ways and means, at the national, regional and international levels, to eliminate violence against women and its causes, and to remedy its consequences." Finally, she is asked to work closely with the UN Commission on the Status of Women as well as other special rapporteurs, independent experts, working groups, and treaty bodies under the auspices of the Commission on Human Rights. All of these developments reflect significant responses from the international human rights community to the demands of the Global Campaign for Women's Human Rights. The task of implementing such measures in an effective manner is a complex and difficult one, which requires continued vigilance and political mobilization on the part of women's groups and human right's organizations.

Chapter 11
Implementing Women's Human Rights After Vienna

The Global Campaign for Women's Human Rights was successful beyond the expectations of most of its organizers in raising the profile of women's human rights. It was also an important learning experience for those involved, most of whom had little prior experience working with UN machineries. The challenge now is to translate that success and experience into long term advances in the implementation of women's human rights on an everyday basis, from the local to the global level.

In its early stages of development, the Global Campaign made the strategic decision to emphasize issues of gender-based violence as ones which best illustrate how traditional human rights concepts and practice are gender-biased and exclude a large spectrum of women's human rights abuse. Since different forms of violence against women clearly parallel other types of human rights violation that the international community has condemned, such as torture, enslavement, terrorism, etc., they were a useful starting point for showing concretely the meaning of a gender perspective on human rights. Unfortunately, some people interpreted this strategy as lack of concern for other types of human rights abuse suffered by women. This was further complicated by the media, which primarily reported on the violence aspects of the Global Tribunal and almost universally ignored the testimonies of socio-economic violations that were reported there. One of the challenges now faced by the "women's rights as human rights" movement is to work simultaneously to implement the promises made to women in Vienna around gender-based violence (an enormous task in itself), and at the same time to strengthen the understanding that women's human rights concerns include other issues, such as health, socio-economic rights, and racial justice.

The first post-Vienna action by the Global Campaign for Women's Human Rights, announced at a press briefing sponsored by UNIFEM on the last day of the Conference, was to establish a new timetable demanding that the United Nations report on progress made toward implementing the *Vienna Declaration* at the time of the UN Fourth World Conference on Women (WCW) to be held in Beijing in September 1995. Toward that end, the petition campaign which had served as such a useful organizing tool to get women at the local level engaged in the process before Vienna, continues. The new version of the petition quotes the *Vienna Declaration* as well as the *Universal Declaration of Human Rights*, and calls upon the UN to report in Beijing on concrete efforts made to implement women's human rights (see *Part IV, Document A*). It is intended, as the initial petition has done, to serve as a local organizing and educational tool to inform women about the *Vienna Declaration* and other international human rights promises made to them. This will encourage more women to learn about and demand their rights, and to use international human rights language and documents in their local and national organizing for change.

The second objective of the petition is to keep the UN and national governments aware that women are watching to see how they will deliver on the promises they made in Vienna. This human rights monitoring goes beyond just the petition drive to include active training of women in human rights procedures and methods of documentation, and efforts to expand women's participation in various human rights meetings and bodies regionally and internationally. A number of organizations are now conducting training activities and are working to get more women involved. Some projects are also aimed specifically at human rights education for women, such as the Global Campaign of Human Rights Education on Women's Human Rights and Gender Equality, an NGO initiative directed toward the UN Decade of Human Rights Education which begins in 1995.

The annual campaign of *16 Days of Activism Against Gender Violence*, which is now in its fourth year, has expanded to more countries, many of whom are utilizing the new petition and the *Vienna Declaration* to draw attention to the human rights dimensions of violence against women. The *16 Days* campaign seeks to demonstrate how gender-based violence is linked to other aspects of women's human rights abuse in areas like migration, poverty, and reproductive health. The Global Campaign is also continuing to encourage local and regional hearings and tribunals to expose and document the human rights abuse that females suffer. A number of such hearings are scheduled as part of the activities building up to the WCW in Beijing, including an ongoing series of public hearings organized by the Asian Women's Human Rights Council.

The Center for Women's Global Leadership, in collaboration with some of the other organizations active in the Global Campaign, held a hearing at the International Conference on Population and Development in Cairo in September 1994. Likewise, a hearing will be held at the World Summit on Social Development in Copenhagen, March 1995, in order to increase recognition of the women's human rights dimensions of reproductive health and socio-economic rights. Both of these events will culminate in another global tribunal in Beijing aimed at holding the UN and its member states accountable for the promises that they made to women not only in Vienna, but also in the *Forward Looking Strategies* document at the end of the UN Decade for Women in Nairobi in 1985, and in other documents like the *Convention on the Elimination of All Forms of Discrimination Against Women.* The Beijing Tribunal will form the basis for a report on women's human rights to be presented not only to the WCW in Beijing, but also to the UN on the occasion of its 50th anniversary celebration in October 1995.

Much that was learned from The Tribunal held in Vienna can be applied to other hearings and tribunals in the future. Based on feedback from the testifiers and from many who attended or heard about it, The Global Tribunal on Violations of Women's Human Rights was seen as effective on a variety of levels. First, it provided legitimacy in an international arena for women to articulate and record violations of their human rights that were symbolic of the experiences of hundreds of thousands of women. Second, it deepened the analysis of what constitutes women's human rights, and fostered greater consciousness of gender-based human rights abuse. Third, as a media event, it brought women's human rights issues to wider attention and therefore created more pressure on the UN and governments to listen to women's demands. Fourth, The Tribunal provided a powerful focal event to which diverse women could point in support of their varying claims, and was an empowering occasion for many of the women who testified as well as for those who listened or heard about it later. Finally, The Tribunal became a symbol or metaphor for the long neglected abuses of women and their growing determination to demand accountability for these violations.

However, there are limitations to what a non-governmental or popular tribunal can achieve and it is important to be clear about what can be expected from it. A popular tribunal is primarily a tool to promote public awareness of issues and to invoke political and moral pressure on policy making. It is not a legal process and does not produce recommendations that are legally binding or enforceable. Women who testify must understand this, because for some people a tribunal represents a last hope for justice. For this reason, popular tribunals should strive to present cases which are being actively pursued, legally and/or politically, by local or regional groups. In this way, participation can contribute to the political momentum of a social movement without raising false expectations for an individual testifier.

Further, while exposing women's victimization in this manner is a critical step toward eliminating violations, it is equally important not to represent women only as victims. Therefore, the testimonies also need to highlight efforts organizations are making to counter the human rights abuse described in their accounts. This dimension of a hearing can be enhanced if it is systematically linked to subsequent workshops, events or actions. In doing so, those who testify and listen can strategize more concretely about how to transform existing human rights practice so that female human rights abuse is considered.

The impact of The Global Tribunal on Violations of Women's Human Rights in Vienna was considerable. Women who testified there or as part of ongoing hearings elsewhere are helping to dismantle the wall of silence that has long surrounded gender-based human rights abuse. This is a critical part of creating the political climate necessary for realization of women's rights as human rights.

Legal Redress and Human Rights Documentation

The promotion and protection of human rights involves both political and legal strategies. Much of the Global Campaign for Women's Human Rights has been focused on the political—developing a conceptual understanding of how gender affects human rights, exposing the neglect of violations against women, and creating the political will to do something about them. As a greater understanding of the human rights of women is developing and the political pressure to address them grows, there is increasing need for more work on the legal aspects of these issues.

Documentation is critical to actively pursuing legal redress for human rights abuses and to giving definition to violations previously ignored even by human rights practitioners. The Global Campaign and the various hearings held have sought to promote the documentation of gender-based violations in order to make them visible as human rights issues. When such documentation takes place in the context of a speakout, hearing, or tribunal, it can also play the political role of promoting greater human rights awareness and mobilization. In addition, the documentation process can also reveal patterns of violations which affect women across social, economic, cultural and geographic boundaries, thereby strengthening women's demands for their human rights as a group.

Beyond holding hearings, other important work has been done that illustrates how to document gender specific human rights abuse in a legal context. For example, several organizations have documented rape and forced pregnancy in Bosnia as part of the effort to demand accountability for war crimes there. Amnesty International has recorded and campaigned against rape in custody as a form of torture. Creative work has been done by the Women's Rights Project of Human Rights Watch, in collaboration with local women's organizations, to produce innovative accounts of the state's responsibility for human rights violations in areas like trafficking in women from Burma to Thailand, domestic violence in Brazil, and virginity control in Turkey. The director of this project, Dorothy Q. Thomas, has posed the challenges of documentation succinctly by noting that work must be done to describe and prove clearly:

▶ what is the violation;

▶ who is the violator; and

▶ what is the remedy sought.[1]

Given the inter-connected nature of many violations that women suffer, and

---

[1] For a fuller description of Dorothy Thomas' presentation on this topic, see the report of the 3rd Women's Global Leadership Institute to be published by the Center for Women's Global Leadership in late 1994. The most recent reports of the Human Rights Watch Women's Project are listed in *Part IV, Document H.*

the ways in which public and private intersect in women's lives, this is not always easy to do.

Formal processes for filing legal complaints of human rights abuses for the purpose of achieving redress are constrained on a number of levels. Documentation submitted for consideration to UN international human rights bodies must name the state or states responsible for the violations. Where violations or patterns of human rights abuse do not result from direct state action, but from the state's failure to take preventative action or to actively ensure justice, it can be difficult to establish state responsibility and to clarify just who is the violator. A complaint is more readily processed and a ruling of human rights abuse given when the violations are carried out by individuals acting as state agents, as in cases of arbitrary arrest or torture in police or military custody. Yet, as the testimonies at The Vienna Tribunal indicate, while such violations do happen to women and are often gender-specific, much of the human rights abuse women experience occurs at the hands of non-state actors, whether private individuals or religious institutions, and in the context of the private spheres of family, economy, culture, and religion. Yet, even the *UN International Covenant on Economic, Social, and Cultural Rights (ICESCR)*, which most explicitly sets out to guarantee human rights in these arenas, is a weak human rights mechanism in terms of establishing accountability and achieving remedial action. It is crucial, therefore, to establish that the state is responsible for seeking to prevent and for punishing non-state actors who violate the human rights of women, just as it is responsible for preventing non-state actors from engaging in activities like slavery or para-military death squads.

A further limitation in using a particular covenant or treaty legally is that the state in question must have ratified it, and must be cooperating with the treaty body that oversees compliance, in order to be held accountable to its standards. Also, when individuals are submitting complaints in reference to specific covenants, they must show that they have exhausted all domestic remedies before appealing internationally. Nevertheless, where a situation exists which is recognized as constituting a pattern of "gross violation," then the international human rights community can take action on the grounds that the conditions in question undermine the tenets of the *Universal Declaration of Human Rights* which every state is morally bound to uphold.

The following overview briefly describes UN complaints procedures that are available to individuals who have been subject to human rights violations.[2] One such procedure is the "optional protocol." The "optional protocol" affords the greatest degree of public accountability and effectiveness. It allows the UN Human Rights Committee, which oversees the *UN International Covenant on Civil and Political Rights (ICPCR)*, to receive communications from individuals who claim that their human rights have been violated by a state. However, the Human Rights Committee can only process non-anonymous complaints from individuals of those states that have signed and ratified the *ICPCR* and its Optional Protocol, and where the complaints pertain to violations of human rights covered by that covenant. Once a case satisfies the Committee's criteria, the person making the complaint will be informed of, and may respond to, developments along the way including responses made by the state in question. The entire process may take up to three years to produce a ruling.

The fact that the civil and political covenant has such an optional protocol, while other human rights instruments like the economic, social and cultural covenant and the women's convention do not, underscores the tacit hierarchy of human rights practice. Further, the rights delineated in the *ICESCR* are qualified as aspirations to be achieved over time so that violations—even when fatal or life threatening—are not treated as urgent. This prioritization represents a particular obstacle for women who wish to document and remedy violations of their human rights which are per-petrated in the name of culture or religion, or are the result of gender-based economic exploitation. Nonetheless, both the Committee on Economic, Social and Cultural Rights and the Committee on the Elimination of Discrimination Against Women, who oversee these two conventions, do receive country reports from states that have ratified them and encourage alternative reports from individuals and non-governmental organizations pertaining to violations of the conventions. Not only can such submissions influence the policy recommendations and official state-ments of international bodies, but they may also shame the government involved into taking action on a particular case or issue.

The second major avenue to register complaints of human rights abuse is the "1503" procedure, which allows the Sub-Commission on Prevention of Discrimi-nation and Protection of Minorities to receive first- and second-hand reports of any "consistent pattern of gross violations of human rights and fundamental free-

---

[2] See *Part IV, Document G* for chart mapping out the Human Rights bodies of the United Nations.

doms...affecting a large number of people over a protracted period of time" (*Human Rights Communications Procedures,* UN Fact Sheet no. 7). Under the "1503" procedure, an individual, group, or non-governmental organization can submit a report of gross violations affecting a group of people. The Sub-Commission may then decide to enter into dialogue with the state or states in question, undertake a thorough investigation based on the complaint, establish a thematic working group, and/or appoint a special rapporteur.

In addition, the Committees overseeing the *UN Convention on the Elimination of Racial Discrimination* and the *UN Convention against Torture* can receive individual communications regarding human rights abuses. The Commission on the Status of Women also prepares two lists each year of human rights violations affecting women, one of which is public and the other confidential. Two of the UN specialized agencies, the International Labour Office (ILO) and the United Nations Educational, Scientific and Cultural Organization (UNESCO), have also created international legislation in defense of human rights within their mandated areas and supervise its implementation.

Furthermore, there are dozens of thematic and/or regional special rapporteurs, representatives, and working groups within the UN human rights machinery which depend upon non-governmental sources to carry out their investigations into human rights abuse. These special procedures cover topics such as discrimination against AIDS/HIV infected individuals, violations relating to extreme poverty, indigenous peoples' rights, human rights abuse in occupied territories, and several with gender specific mandates such as the Working Group on Contemporary Forms of Slavery, the Special Rapporteur on Traditional Practices Affecting the Health of Women and Children, and now the Rapporteur on Violence Against Women. Another result of women's lobbying over the past few years is the effort now underway to establish an "optional protocol" to the *Convention on the Elimination of All Forms of Discrimination Against Women,* which would allow individual complaints of violations of its tenets to be heard.

Despite clear constraints, the procedures outlined above represent important opportunities to make formal reports and legal complaints regarding violations of the human rights of women. Every such opportunity also affords the political possibility of making female human rights abuse more visible and less acceptable. Even though achieving legal accountability and redress is a difficult task, there are many avenues within the UN and regional human rights machineries through which human rights policy can be influenced and transformed, and particular incidents of human rights abuse condemned. Developing a human rights framework from a gender perspective means using multiple means to demand accountability for violations of women's human rights, including legal measures, political pressure, and moral suasion.

Integrating Gender into Human Rights Theory and Practice

When governments agreed to address the human rights of women in the *Vienna Declaration*, there was greater acceptance of the separate section on women's specific human rights than on the inclusion of gender perspectives and women as a dimension in other areas of human rights. This revealed much about the work ahead in seeking to promote and protect the full range of women's human rights. The first task of the Global Campaign was to show that there are gender-specific human rights violations that have been neglected because they are acts exclusively or primarily done to women, in areas such as reproduction and sexual violence. While this work must continue, an equally or even more difficult task ahead is to demonstrate how other human rights concerns are affected by gender.

For example, how one experiences ethnic violence or torture in prison is usually affected by both gender and race. This is not to say that women's experience is worse than men's but it is usually different. If human rights practice assumes the male experience as generic, much of what happens to women is made invisible or merely added as an afterthought rather than taken into account as a central part of shaping definitions of abuse and remedies for it. Thus, for example, policies dealing with political prisoners, migrants, or refugees must take into account that for women, sexual violence, or the threat of it, is almost always a central part of their experience in these situations.

The realization of women's human rights requires not only that *CEDAW* and gender-specific mechanisms be implemented but that, in addition, other treaties like the *ICCPR* and the *ICESCR* are utilized to benefit women. One of the most important and challenging aspects of the *Vienna Declaration*, therefore, is the recognition that "The equal status of women and the human rights of women should be integrated into the mainstream of United Nations system-wide activity.

These issues should be regularly and systematically addressed throughout relevant United Nations bodies and mechanisms"(paragraph 37). The *Declaration* recognizes that this call for the integration of women and gender perspectives into United Nations human rights machinery will not happen automatically, but requires special attention from its various bodies. Specific measures to achieve such integration are suggested, such as the recommendations that treaty-monitoring bodies use "gender-specific data," that states "supply information on the situation of women de jure and de facto in their reports," and that the UN provide training for its "human rights and humanitarian relief personnel to assist them to recognize and deal with human rights abuses particular to women and to carry out their work without gender bias" (paragraph 42).

At its 50th session in February of 1994, the UN Commission on Human Rights reaffirmed these objectives from the *Vienna Declaration* in a broad resolution on "Integrating the rights of women into the human rights mechanisms of the United Nations" (B/CN.4/1994/L.8/Rev.1). Sponsored by over 50 countries from all regions, the resolution demonstrated once more that governments feel they must at least appear to be responding to the demands for action around the human rights of women. The resolution asks all UN human rights treaty bodies, working groups, commissions, rapporteurs, and experts to consider the gender specific aspects of their topics and to "regularly and systematically include in their reports available information on human rights violations affecting women." The UN Centre for Human Rights is charged with overseeing this integration, and specifically with providing the gender training for human rights personnel outlined in the *Vienna Declaration.*

If all of these measures were implemented, great strides would be made toward realizing the integration of women into human rights practice. The problem is that neither the United Nations nor most member states have allocated significant resources toward the achievement of these objectives. To date, the UN Centre for Human Rights has reassigned an existing staff person to be the "focal point" for women, and little has yet been done to see that all personnel, male and female, receive the gender awareness training needed to understand and develop ways of adapting traditional human rights practice to meet women's specific needs. If these objectives are to be met, women must not only keep the political pressure on both governments and the UN, but must also develop documentation, guidelines, and case studies that demonstrate what it means to integrate gender into all areas of human rights. For example, important work can be done to show how women's freedom of expression is systematically curtailed both by members of their families and by religious forces that seek to keep women out of the public sphere. To take another case, documentation can be gathered on the ways in which states and international monetary institutions discriminate against women and violate their human right to food and shelter.

Such a full integration will require changes in human rights theory and application of concepts as well as in human rights practice. Many human rights documents state non-discrimination as a principle, but the interpretation of their basic tenets is usually shaped by the experiences of the males who have traditionally dominated this field. For example, the *Universal Declaration of Human Rights* asserts that everyone has the right to "security of person" and to not be subjected to "cruel, inhuman or degrading treatment." Read from the perspective of women's lives, it seems clear that an issue like violence against women should be included under such a concept. Yet, it has taken over 40 years for such a woman-centred reading to begin to be understood and accepted, at least rhetorically, by women as well as men. Such is the depth of the hidden gender-bias that has affected the definitions of which human rights will be promoted and protected. Only as more women become fully involved in defining and documenting the variety of female experiences of human rights abuse will this imbalance be corrected and the full range of both female and male human rights abuses be addressed.

While it is encouraging that many gender-specific human rights abuses are being acknowledged for the first time, these gains are also being accompanied by intense resistance to the realization of women's rights as human rights. Most recently this has been evident in the events surrounding the UN International Conference on Population and Development in Cairo (September, 1994). At that meeting, many NGOs supporting women succeeded in firmly linking any future discussion of population policy to considerations of women's human rights. However, this was achieved in the context of severe opposition from fundamentalist religious forces, both Christian and Muslim. This made ever more clear that the attack on the human rights of women has moved to the forefront of the opposition to the universality of human rights. Yet, supporters of women's human rights in Cairo still had to contend with complaints from some participants that the emphasis on women's status detracted attention from "more important" consid-erations such as environmental destruction and over-consumption in the North. It is now more critical than ever to emphasize that the defense of the human rights of women not only protects the birthright of half of humanity, but also forms the basis of the realization of human rights for all in the 21st century.

Part IV
Campaign Documents and Resources

Document A
Petition to the United Nations to Promote and Protect the Human Rights of Women

the GLOBAL
CAMPAIGN *for*
WOMEN'S
HUMAN
RIGHTS

After Vienna and on to Beijing
The Global Campaign for Women's Human Rights Continues...

The Universal Declaration of Human Rights protects everyone "without distinction of any kind such as race, colour, sex, language...or other status" (art. 2). Further, everyone has the right to "life, liberty and security of person" (art. 3) and "no one shall be subject to torture or to cruel, inhuman or degrading treatment" (art. 5). In addition, the 1993 Vienna Declaration of the World Conference on Human Rights states that the "human rights of women and of the girl-child are an inalienable, integral and indivisible part of universal human rights," and declares a commitment to eliminate "violence against women in public and private life." Therefore, we, the undersigned, call upon the United Nations to fulfill this commitment and to report on its efforts to promote and protect women's human rights at the Fourth World Conference on Women (Beijing, September 1995).

Name	Address
1.	
2.	
3.	
4.	
5.	
6.	
7.	
8.	
9.	
10.	
11.	
12.	
13.	
14.	

Please copy and return forms to: Center for Women's Global Leadership, 27 Clifton Avenue, Douglass College, New Brunswick, NJ 08903 USA. Fax: 1.908.932.1180 or International Women's Tribune Centre, 777 UN Plaza, New York, NY 10017, USA. Fax: 1.212.661.2704. Deadline for receipt of petitions is July 31, 1995. Write for more information or to receive a full list of sponsors.

Partial List of International and Regional Sponsoring Groups for the Petition:

Center for Women's Global Leadership; IWTC; World YWCA; Abolitionist Fed.; Bahai'i International; DAWN (Development Alternatives with Women for a New Era); FIRE; Institute for Women, Law and Development; ISIS-International (Manila); ISIS-International (Santiago); ISIS-WICCE (Geneva); International Alliance of Women; International Assoc. of Women in Radio and Television; International Center for Law and Development; International Centre for Human Rights and Democratic Development; Internatinal Council of Jewish Women; International Council of Women; International Fed. of Business and Professional Women; International Fed. of University Women; International Women's Rights Action Watch; International Inner Wheel Clubs; International Peace and Research Assoc.; International Union of Students; International Women's Health Coalition; International Women's Human Rights Law Clinic; MATCH International Centre; Organizing Committee for Decade on Human Rights Education; WIDF; Women's International League for Peace and Freedom; Third World Movement Against the Exploitation of Women; Women for Racial and Economic Equality; Women's Global Network for Reproductive Rights; Women's International Democratic Fed.; Women Living Under Muslim Laws; World Confederation of Organizations of the Teaching Profession; World Federalist Assoc.; World Fed. of Methodist Women; World Union of Catholic Women's Organization; Women's Environment and Development Organization (WEDO); Women's Exchange Program International; World University Service; Zonta International. Regional Groups: African Centre for Democracy and Human Rights; African Participatory Research Network; Arab Women's Solidarity Assoc.; Asociación Latinoamericana para los Derechos Humanos; Asian Women Human Rights Council; Assoc. of African Women for Research and Development; Asia Pacific Forum on Women, Law and Development; Beirut University College; Caribbean Assoc. for Feminist Research and Action (CAFRA); Comité Latinoamericano para la Defensa de los Derechos de la Mujer (CLADEM); European Union of Women; Asociación Interamericana de Servicios Legales (ILSA); Mujer/Fempress; Pacific Women's Resource Bureau; PPSEAW; Soroptimist International; Women in Development Europe (WIDE); Women in Law and Development Africa (WiLDAF); Women in Law in Southern Africa Research Project; Worldview International Foundation (and over 1000 local or national organizations).

Document B
Hearings, Speakouts, and Tribunals Around the World

In 1991, the Center for Women's Global Leadership launched the first annual campaign of *16 Days of Activism against Gender Violence*. This *16 Days* campaign inspired the Global Center and the International Women's Tribune Centre to start a worldwide petition drive calling upon the United Nations to comprehensively address violations of women's human rights as it prepared for the first World Conference on Human Rights in 25 years.[1] The petition proved to be an effective mobilizing, educational, and lobbying tool to advance women's human rights. In order to build on this momentum, the second *16 Days* in 1992 called for international hearings to document female human rights abuse.[2] The call was also made in solidarity with the Asian Women's Human Rights Council, which was planning a series of public hearings in the Asia-Pacific region to follow the World Conference on Human Rights in Vienna and leading up to the UN Fourth World Conference on Women (WCW). The following is an account of some of the hearings, speakouts and tribunals that the Center has heard about since the second *16 Days* campaign which have contributed to making violations of women's human rights more visible.

The Center for Women's Global Leadership and the YWCA of Central New Jersey launched the second *16 Days* campaign locally with a hearing on November 24,

---

[1] At the UN World Conference on Human Rights, participants in the Global Campaign for Women's Human Rights presented a third round of signatures to the Conference plenary, bringing the total delivered close to half a million. The petition had been translated into 23 languages, and signatures came from 124 countries. The petition now has more than 1000 sponsoring groups, and the revised version demands that the United Nations and its member states report on the measures they are taking to implement human rights for women at the UN Fourth World Conference on Women in Beijing in 1995.

[2] As part of the hearings campaign, the Center for Women's Global Leadership and the International Women's Tribune Centre developed a *Form for Documenting Violations of Women's Human Rights* and guidelines for holding a hearing. Both are reproduced in *International Campaign for Women's Human Rights* 1992-1993 Report (Center for Women's Global Leadership, 1993), and in *"A Call To Action!"* (IWTC, March 1993).

1992 in New Brunswick, New Jersey, USA. Seven women testified on violations of women's human rights in the United States. They emphasized the ways in which sexism, racism, and poverty, as well as discrimination in the judiciary and in the provision of social services, serve as major obstacles to securing the human rights of women.

In Secunderabad, India, on December 1-2, 1992, the Asmita Resource Centre for Women convened a two day forum on gender violence and human rights. The forum was attended by 2000 women, and included a speakout where women protested child marriages, family violence, dowry murder, and economic exploitation in the home and society (See *Part IV, Document H* for information to get a full report of this event).

Following the launch of the international hearings campaign, many organizations began to plan hearings for 1993. On February 19, 1993, the Center for Women's Global Leadership, the International Women's Tribune Centre, and the United Methodist United Nations Office held an international hearing in New York City which featured testimonies from countries such as Sudan, Burma, Philippines, and the United States. The 15 speakers addressed violations of women's human rights in the context of militarism and fundamentalism, including specific abuses pertaining to rape and ethnic cleansing in the former Yugoslavia, lesbian persecution, trafficking, female genital mutilation, immigrant and refugee procedures, and UN personnel policies that condone spousal abuse. Many who testified were active in the Global Campaign for Women's Human Rights and reported on actions being taken in their regions to stem violations of women's human rights. A panel of four judges active in UN processes concluded the hearing with comments on how they would address women's human rights in both NGO and UN work.

To mark International Women's Day, March 8, 1993, the Center for Immigration and Refugee Rights and Services, in conjunction with the Family Violence Prevention Fund, organized a Public Hearing Documenting Human Rights Abuses Against Immigrant and Refugee Women in the United States. Held in San Francisco, this event included more than 11 speakers originally from countries such as Chile, Mexico, China, Haiti, and the Philippines. The women recounted stories of economic servitude, physical and mental abuse, sexual harassment, and rape at the hands of their employers without recourse to legal protection or redress.

On March 25, the Human Rights Center at the State University of New York at Buffalo, along with the International Institute of Buffalo and VIVE Inc. (an organization for world refugees), co-sponsored a hearing to document violations of women's human rights around the world, including the United States. The nine cases presented addressed violence in the home, violations against immigrant and refugee women in the United States, and harmful traditional practices.

A Victim Women's Forum, was convened by the Informal Sector Service Centre in Nepal from February 12-15, 1993. The Forum sought to raise consciousness among women in Nepal about the abuse of their human rights, and to encourage strategies to combat the violations. The event also aimed to "bring out the hidden victimizing system and oppression [of] women, so that they will get wider coverage in the press."[3] The Forum presented 16 cases addressing such violations as those experienced by women workers, bonded women, trafficked women, and women victims of family violence. The public hearing was accompanied by group discussions which produced sets of recommendations to end the human rights abuse that had been documented at the Forum.

Following The Global Tribunal at the World Conference on Human Rights in Vienna, June 1993, a number of groups began to plan hearings and tribunals, (many of which are not reported here because the Center has not received documentation from them, although we have heard that they were held). At the regional level, a Tribunal was held at the Feminist Encuentro for Latin America and the Caribbean in El Salvador in early November 1993. A video documenting this event, *Rompiendo Fronteras*, is available from FIRE—Feminist International Radio Endeavor in Costa Rica (see *Part IV, Document H*).

During the *16 Days* campaign in 1993, several hearings were convened around the world in countries such as Argentina, Pakistan, and Zambia. In Rosario, Argentina, three organizations—Indeso Mujer, Casa de la Mujer, and Mujer Marcha—convened a public tribunal on November 25. The speakers were women's advocates who presented five cases on behalf of women and girls who had been subject to sexual violence, battery and murder, psychological torture culminating in suicide, economic violence, and military rape. The cases were heard by members of the judiciary, who then made recommendations regarding changes required both in the law and in cultural mores and attitudes toward women.

---

[3] *Women's Victim Forum.* INSEC. Nepal, 1993.

In Lusaka, Zambia, the Young Women's Christian Association organized a Tribunal on Violations against Women in the Family. The three hour event took place on December 8, 1993, when 250 people heard 10 women testify to human rights abuses they had suffered at the hands of family members. The seven-person jury, mostly comprised of practicing judges, made a wide-ranging series of recommendations including a call to accept "cumulative provocation" as a "complete defense," and not just a mitigating factor, in cases where women kill their abusive husbands. The judges also urged the incorporation of *CEDAW* into Zambia's national laws.

The Asian Women's Human Rights Council launched its regional hearings campaign in December 1993 with a Public Hearing on Violence against Women in Lahore, Pakistan, which was coordinated by Simorgh. The second Public Hearing on Trafficking and War Crimes against Women took place in Tokyo, March 1994, and was coordinated by 60 Japanese women's groups. Also in March, 1994, Women's Voice of Bangalore coordinated a third Public Hearing on Crimes against Dalit Women in Bangalore, India. The Council convened a fourth Public Hearing on Crimes Against Women related to Population Policy during the International Conference on Population and Development in Cairo, September 1994. Also scheduled are Public Hearings on Development in India, December 1994, on Crimes against Indigenous Women in April 1995, and on Nuclearization and Militarization in May 1995.

Several of the preceding utilized the "Form for Documenting Violations of Women's Human Rights" and forwarded documentation to the Center for Women's Global Leadership, which submitted it to the Geneva-based UN Centre for Human Rights. The Canadian Immigrant and Refugee Board also sent the Center documentation of 15 gender-specific human rights abuse cases affecting immigrant women in Canada. In addition, a number of individuals forwarded details of cases which they wanted presented at the Vienna Conference. Hearings, tribunals and other methods of documenting violations of women's human rights continue to be held and planned by women active in the Global Campaign in many parts of the world, and documentation from this will continue to be sent to the UN Centre for Human Rights to establish that such violations require urgent attention.

Document C
Programme of The Global Tribunal on Violations of Women's Human Rights

9:00-9:30
OPENING
- Charlotte Bunch, Director, Center for Women's Global Leadership
- Johanna Dohnal, Austrian Minister for Women's Affairs
- Marjorie Thorpe, Deputy Director, UNIFEM (UN Development Fund for Women)

9:30-10:50
HUMAN RIGHTS ABUSE IN THE FAMILY
Chair, Monica O'Connor, Irish Women's Aid
- Gayla Thompson, USA
- Perveen Martha, PAKISTAN
- Stella Mukasa for Miss Dravu, UGANDA
- Rosa Logar, AUSTRIA
- Maria Celsa da Conceiçao, BRAZIL
- Sara Patricia Portugués, COSTA RICA
- Gabrielle Wilders, USA
Judge's Statement
Elizabeth Odio, Costa Rica Minister for Justice, member of the UN Committee Against Torture

11:20-12:30
WAR CRIMES AGAINST WOMEN
Chair, Nelia Sancho Liao, Asian Women's Human Rights Council
- Chin Sung Chung and Bok Dong Kim, KOREA
- Randa Siniora, PALESTINE
- M. Asha Samad, SOMALIA
- Ema Hilario, PERU
- Janet Tello Gilardi for Sandra Gonzáles, PERU
- Olga Kudryavtseva, RUSSIA
- Slavica Kušić , CROATIA
- Lepa Mladjenović , SERBIA
- Fadila Memišević & Aida Zaidgiz, BOSNIA/HERZEGOVINA
Judge's Statement
Ed Broadbent, former Canadian MP and President of the International Centre for Human Rights and Democratic Development

14:00-15:00
VIOLATIONS OF BODILY INTEGRITY
Chair, Gladys Acosta, Instituto Latinoamericano de Servicios Legales Alternativos (ILSA)
- Lin Lap-Chew for Grazyna from Poland, THE NETHERLANDS
- Nahid Toubia, SUDAN
- Johanne Gilbert, CANADA
- Rebeca Sevilla, PERU
- Petrona Sandoval, NICARAGUA
Judge's Statement
Justice P.N. Bhagwati, former Chief Justice of the Supreme Court of India and Chair of the Asian human rights NGO AWARE

15:00-16:00
SOCIO-ECONOMIC RIGHTS
Chair, Florence Butegwa, Women in Law and Development in Africa, WiLDAF
- María Lourdes de Jesús, CAPE VERDE/ITALY
- Bernice See, PHILIPPINES
- Charon Asetoyer, USA
- Ayesha Arshad, BANGLADESH
- Elaine Hewitt, BARBADOS
Judge's Statement: Justice P.N. Bhagwati

16:00-16:10
POLITICAL PERSECUTION AND DISCRIMINATION
Chair, Charlotte Bunch, Center for Women's Global Leadership
- María Olea, CHILE/USA
- Gertrude Fester, SOUTH AFRICA
- Norma Valle and Ana Rivera-Lassén, PUERTO RICO
- Khalida Messaoudi for "Oum Ali," ALGERIA
Judge's Statement
Gertrude Mongella, former Tanzanian High Commissioner to India, Secretary-General of the UN Fourth World Conference on Women

Final Judges' Statement
Introduced by Anne Walker, Director, International Women's Tribune Centre

Document D
Report of The Global Tribunal on Violations of Women's Human Rights

Submitted to the World Conference on Human Rights, Vienna 14-25 June 1993

Delivered by: Charlotte Bunch (USA) Director,
Center for Women's Global Leadership Rutgers University
and
Florence Butegwa (Uganda) Coordinator,
Women in Law and Development in Africa (WiLDAF)

On Tuesday, over 1,000 people attended a day-long Global Tribunal on Violations of Women's Human Rights. We heard moving testimony by 33 women from all regions of the world about abuses they have suffered. These accounts demonstrated dramatically that the United Nations and governments have failed to promote and protect women's human rights.

Women testified to specific abuses in five basic areas:

▶ Human Rights Abuses in the Family

▶ War Crimes Against Women

▶ Violations of Women's Bodily Integrity

▶ Violations of Women's Socio-Economic Rights

▶ Political Persecution and Discrimination

This Tribunal was the culmination of an international campaign by over 900 women's organizations around the world seeking to bring women's human rights issues onto the agenda of this Conference. As I speak, women are delivering the signed petitions that started this campaign. This petition has been circulated in

124 countries and translated into 23 languages. It has been signed by almost half a million people. The petition reads:

The Universal Declaration of Human Rights protects everyone "without distinction of any kind such as race, colour, sex, language...or other status" (art. 2). Furthermore, "Everyone has the right to life, liberty and security of person (art. 3) and no one shall be subject to torture or to cruel, inhuman or degrading treatment or punishment" (art. 5). Therefore, we, the undersigned call upon the 1993 United Nations World Conference on Human Rights to comprehensively address women's rights at every level of its proceedings. We demand that gender violence, a universal phenomenon which takes many forms across culture, race and class, be recognized as a violation of human rights requiring immediate action.

In presenting these petitions and reporting on this Tribunal, we ask this body to consider, "Why was such a Tribunal necessary? Why has this area of massive violation of women remained invisible for so long? And what will the world community do to redress this abuse in the future?"

Abuses of women have too long been dismissed as private, family, cultural, or religious matters. Today, we demand that they be seen for what they are: fundamental violations of the "right to life, liberty and security of person," as guaranteed by the Universal Declaration of Human Rights.

Violations of women's rights not only rob us of our own human dignity and freedom, but also cause physical, mental and psychological damage. Millions of women die from these abuses every year.

The Global Campaign for Women's Human Rights, a coalition of women's groups from around the world, organized this one-day Tribunal to bring to you and to the listening world these moving stories of women whose lives have been violated. In doing this, women are tearing down the wall of silence that has prevented the world from recognizing the abuses women face.

We hope this concrete evidence of abuse will galvanize all of you to take decisive action to end such violations.

The coalition would like to present here the conclusions reached by our panel of distinguished judges. They are:

Gertrude Mongella, Secretary-General of the UN Fourth World Conference on Women;

Ed Broadbent, President of the International Centre for Human Rights and Democratic Development in Montreal;

Justice P.N. Bhagwati, former Chief Justice of the Supreme Court of India;

Elizabeth Odio, Minister for Justice in Costa Rica and member of the UN Committee Against Torture.

We submit the recommendations of these judges to you for your urgent action. We hope you will be moved to assume responsibility for defending women's human rights in the 21st century so that the promise of universal human rights will be realized. This is not an appeal on behalf of a special interest group, but rather, a demand to restore the birthright of half of humanity.

In response to the testimony given at The Global Tribunal, a distinguished panel of judges issued the following statement:

We have heard with anguish and profound regret the first-hand testimony of 33 courageous women from all parts of the world. They have borne personal witness before The Global Tribunal on Violations of Women's Human Rights to prove beyond any doubt that violations of women's human rights continue to be cruel and pervasive on a world scale.

These violations remain both unremedied and unrecognized as discriminatory or as affronts to women's human dignity. This widespread failure to recognize, honour and protect women's human rights poses a challenge to the credibility and justice of international human rights law. We note with dismay that international human rights law has not been applied effectively against injustices women experience solely because of their gender.

We hereby affirm the principle of universality that protects all of humanity, including women. Universal human rights standards are rooted in all cultures, religions and traditions, but those cultural, religious and traditional practices that undermine universality and prove harmful to women cannot be tolerated.

The judges then issued the following recommendations:

We call upon this World Conference on Human Rights, the United Nations and

Member States to establish mechanisms to prevent, investigate and provide redress for violations of women's rights. Here are the specific recommendations:

1. The establishment of an International Criminal Court for Women to protect and enforce women's human rights, including the rights to freedom from sexual abuse, mass rape and forced pregnancy in armed conflict;

2. The strengthening and enforcement of the Convention on the Elimination of All Forms of Discrimination Against Women, specifically by:

   ▶ Universal ratification;

   ▶ Withdrawal of all reservations made upon ratification which perpetuate women's subordination;

   ▶ Effective implementation, combined with elimination of cultural, religious and traditional stereotypes and practices which impede implementation;

3. The integration of gender perspectives in all human rights committees established under human rights treaties, to ensure application of all human rights treaties to all forms of subordination of women;

4. Expansion of the work of the United Nations and its specialized agencies for preventing and redressing all violations of women's rights. We recognize that these cruel and pervasive violations of women's rights retard the progress and development of society and can be prevented by treating women fairly and justly;

5. Recognition that many of these violations take place in the private sphere of the family, and that domestic violence is a violation of human rights. We recommend that the 1994 Year of the Family recognize all forms of supportive relationships that exist within and outside institutionalized family arrangements;

6. Adoption by the General Assembly of the Draft Declaration on the Elimination of Violence Against Women; and

7. Establishment of a Special Rapporteur with a broad mandate to investigate violations of women's human rights.

Further, we call upon the non-governmental organizations and the world media to investigate and report all violations of women's human rights, and to help empower women through training to expose denials of justice by individuals and by all organs of the state.

We would like to close by underscoring the cruel and pervasive nature of the violations inflicted upon women. We congratulate the women who testified before us for their courage in bearing witness, and for their determination to give visibility to these violations that occur continuously against the rights of millions of women around the world.

The courage of these women will inspire many other women to speak out and to demand their human rights, and will encourage others to work for vindication. The voices of these women have broken the silence. Their appeal to the world must be heard. It must be recognized, investigated and sanctioned, and the violations of their human rights must be redressed.

Document E
Position Paper of the Working Group on Women's Rights of the NGO Forum at the World Conference on Human Rights

Vienna, 14-25 June 1993

Women throughout the world have been engaged in organizing and preparing at the local, regional and international levels for the World Conference on Human Rights. This has included, inter alia:

▶ Women in over 124 countries circulating a Petition calling for the inclusion of women in all aspects of the proceedings and deliberations for the World Conference on Human Rights, and specifically for the recognition of gender-based violence as a human rights violation. More than 500,000 signatures have been gathered to date;

▶ Holding hearings on women's human rights issues and abuses in their own countries and regions;

▶ Organizing caucuses and meetings at the regional level and producing documents for their regional meetings;

▶ Reviewing and appraising United Nations instruments, policies, mechanisms, programmes and actions in order to ascertain the progress in the promotion and respect for women's human rights.

Through this organizing and preparation women have come to a number of conclusions regarding their status and conditions, and have developed recommendations for action.

As the Committee on the Elimination of All Forms of Discrimination Against Women stated, "Women continue to be discriminated against all over the world as regards the recognition, enjoyment and exercise of their individual rights in public and in private [life] and are subject to many different forms of violence," and "demand that the violations [of women's human rights] should be combated with greater efficacy by the United Nations programme on the promotion and protection of human rights." (E/CN.6/1993/CRP.2)

Further, as the Commission on the Status of Women expressed, "The prohibition of discrimination on the basis of sex is a part of all human rights instruments. Underdevelopment, certain social and traditional practices and cultural patterns, and all forms of violence and extremism create obstacles to the full realization by women of all of their rights. Human rights are universal and should apply to women and men equally. Violations of the human rights of women have not been fully dealt with by the overall mechanisms of human rights instruments, the means for recourse in the case of violations are not adequate, and the process of achieving de facto equality has been slow." (E/CN.6/1993/1.5)

As women in a series of sub-regional meetings held in Africa concluded, "In spite of the ratification of international and regional human rights instruments, States still maintain laws and practices which discriminate against women. Selective traditions and customs are used by States to perpetuate discrimination against women and to condone it in the private sphere, contrary to obligations freely assumed by States and to the expectations of the international community. This is particularly true in the field of access to land and other economic resources, legal status and capacity and rights within the family."

As the Latin American women in their Regional Preparatory Conference stated, "We denounce as violations against women's human rights any direct or indirect action or omission perpetrated by the State or by individuals in the public or private spheres, which are inflicted upon women during any state of their lives, which have as their object or result in any physical, sexual, psychological or emotional suffering, cause damage to their integrity or their human dignity, deny them the right to self-determination in any sphere of their lives, and any diminution of the sense of security of person, their self-esteem, their capabilities and their personality."

As some 240 participants from 110 non-governmental organizations concerned with issues of human rights and democratic development in the Asia-Pacific region stated, "The issue of women's rights has not been visible in the human rights discourse, in human rights institutions and practices. Patriarchy, which operates through gender, class, caste and ethnicity, is integral to the problems facing women. Patriarchy is a form of slavery and must be eradicated. Women's rights must be addressed in both the public and private spheres of society, in particular in the family. To provide women with a life with dignity and self-determination, it is important that women have inalienable, equal economic rights (e.g. rights to agricultural land, housing and other resources and property). It is imperative for governments and the United Nations to guarantee these rights. Crimes against women, including rape, sexual slavery and trafficking, and domestic violence are rampant. Crimes against women are crimes against humanity, and the failure of governments to prosecute those responsible for such crimes implies complicity."

Though women of Europe, North America, Australia and New Zealand did not meet in a formal series of sub-regional meetings, women in these countries also experience oppression that is based on their gender and compounded by oppression that is connected to many other forms of discrimination and subordination. For example, indigenous women experience the impact of colonialism and racism as well as sexism. Also, women who come from countries which were colonized by Western powers experience the continuing effects of colonization when living in the West, as well as discrimination and exploitation based on their sex. In general, Western women experience systematic discrimination in employment and education, in the justice system, in political life, and in access to adequate health care. Violence against women is of epidemic proportion. Also, despite living in so-called developed countries, many women are poor, and both they and their children suffer the complex and damaging effects of poverty on their health, education and self-respect. In Western societies, women are subordinate to men in both the public and private spheres. They have less power, less status, less income, less security, and less control over their bodies and their lives.

In all regions, it has been found that the United Nations and governments have, by and large, failed to promote and protect women's human rights, whether civil and political, or economic, social and cultural. Women's subordination throughout the world should be recognized as a human rights violation with due account to those structures of oppression that intersect and compound such subordination. Examples of such oppressive structures include those based on race, ethnicity, national origin, class, colonialism, age, sexual orientation, disability, culture, geography, immigration or refugee status, and other considerations. The full realization of women's human rights requires the elimination of all forms of discrimination and the achievement of equality for all women.

Therefore the Women's Working Group urges the United Nations and governments to take the following measures to ensure that women's human rights are systematically recognized in all areas of the United Nation's work, in each and every article of the Covenants and instruments of human rights, and within the self-determination of communities, minorities, indigenous peoples and other peoples, as well as in State institutions.

1. In order to promote the equal realization of women's civil, political, economic, social and cultural rights, we urge the appointment of a Special Rapporteur on the human rights of women through the Commission on Human Rights. The Rapporteur should be authorized to receive and report on information from governments, non-governmental organizations and inter-governmental institutions, to respond effectively to allegations of violations against women, and to recommend measures to prevent continuing violations. The Rapporteur should also report to the Commission on the Status of Women to assist their policy-making function. While we welcome the decision of the Commission on Human Rights to consider the appointment of a Special Rapporteur on violence against women, the Rapporteur's mandate should include systematic gender discrimination, all forms of sexual exploitation, and trafficking in women, and be addressed to all aspects of women's human rights. Violence against women is closely linked to structural inequalities between women and men and there is a critical need for reporting on gender discrimination in all nation states, including those not party to the *Convention on the Elimination of All Forms of Discrimination Against Women (CEDAW).*

2. The implementation procedures under the *Convention on the Elimination of All Forms of Discrimination Against Women* should be strengthened and therefore we recommend the following:

▶ Call upon governments who have not yet ratified CEDAW to do so immediately.

▶ Encourage governments to withdraw those reservations to CEDAW which are obstacles to its effective implementation and to object to reservations by other states parties that are incompatible with the object and purpose of the Convention.

▶ Call for expeditious review of the compatibility of reservations under CEDAW and remove those reservations determined to be incompatible with the principles and spirit of the Convention.

▶ Establish a working group to outline procedures for drafting an optional protocol to develop an individual and group complaints procedure under CEDAW and support the adoption of such a protocol.

▶ Expand the resources of the Committee on the Elimination of All Forms of Discrimination Against Women, which is charged with overseeing the governmental implementation of CEDAW, to enable it to carry out its mandate by authorizing extended meeting sessions, more support staff, other forms of financial and structural support, and action to increase public awareness of CEDAW and the various Recommendations of the Committee at the international, national and regional levels.

▶ Call upon states to effectively implement CEDAW and the various Recommendations of the Committee through the elimination of discriminatory laws, policies, practices, religious prejudices and customs, and through the implementation of positive measures necessary to advance the equality of women. States should present a plan of action which includes monitoring mechanisms at country and local levels. States should also circulate their reports internally, particularly to non-governmental organizations (NGOs) active in the field of women's human rights.

3. All United Nations treaty committees, thematic and country rapporteurs and working groups, independent experts and all bodies entrusted with protecting human rights should address violations of women's human rights by including gender-specific abuses in the areas that fall within their mandates (through advisory services and training programmes, reporting, monitoring and complaints procedures, etc.). Measures to carry out this charge include:

▶ Support training for all United Nations personnel and independent experts to ensure that they will address the full range of human rights abuses specific to women and carry out their work without bias against women.

▶ Enable the Programme on Advisory Services in Human Rights to assist in the integration of a gender-perspective in all this work.

▶ Ensure periodic evaluations of the effectiveness of the United Nations monitoring, reporting and complaints procedures, as well as its advisory services
and training programmes, in addressing and devising more effective responses
to violations of women's human rights.

▶ Call upon each body to prepare a report on the effectiveness of these initiatives
for the 1995 World Conference on Women to be produced in cooperation with
NGOs active in the field.

**4. In reviewing progress made in the field of human rights since the adoption of
the Universal Declaration of Human Rights and in considering the challenges to
the full realization of the human rights of women and men, governments should
consider violence against women.** We note with concern the failure of States,
treaty-based bodies and human rights NGOs to effectively address such violence.
Women all over the world are subjected to certain forms of violence, including
battering in the home, rape, and sexual slavery, because they are women. This systematic and structural violence threatens and denies women their fundamental
rights to life, to security of the person, and to freedom from slavery and slave-like
practices, and it amounts to cruel and inhuman treatment. It is an extreme form of
sex discrimination that denies women the dignity and integrity inherent in the
human person and impairs their capacity to exercise and enjoy other civil and
political, social and economic rights. Women are also subject to violence in the
form of various retrograde customary practices, including genital mutilation,
dowry deaths, and child marriages. Therefore we urge the following:

▶ The World Conference should recommend effective United Nations implementation procedures to eliminate the violence against women that is
endemic to all societies. Various forms of violence against women and sexual
exploitation breach guarantees established in the Universal Declaration, the
Convention on the Elimination of All Forms of Discrimination Against Women,
and other human rights instruments. Such rights include the right not to be
arbitrarily deprived of life, liberty and security of the person; the right not to be
subject to torture or other cruel, inhuman and degrading treatment; the right to
just and favorable conditions of work; the right to equal protection of the law;
and the right to be free from all forms of gender discrimination, including sexual apartheid which results in the division of public space into separate areas
for men and for women. All appropriate treaty bodies and human rights organizations should address gender-based violence as an aspect of these issues.

▶ The World Conference should recognize specifically that gender violence against women in both the private and public spheres is a violation of human rights and constitutes the gravest form of sexual discrimination. Governments have a responsibility to enforce or create new measures to prevent and respond to violence against women and sexual exploitation in both these spheres, including affirmative measures to elimination the conditions that breed this violence.

▶ We welcome the elaboration of the Draft Declaration on Violence Against Women, adopted by the 37th Session of the Commission on the Status of Women, and urge the adoption of this Declaration by the General Assembly as a step toward more comprehensive and enforceable instruments.

▶ The World Conference should recognize discrimination and violence against women based on sexual orientation as a violation of human rights, and incorporate this issue into instruments defending human rights and into the work of United Nations bodies.

5. The massive and escalating sexual exploitation of women by local and global sex industries constitutes a fundamental violation of human rights and a barrier to women's equality. Prostitution, sex tourism, trafficking in women, and other practices that reduce women to sexual commodities have had a particularly devastating impact on women in developing countries and on oppressed groups of women in so-called developed countries. Sexual exploitation is cruel, inhuman, and degrading, and is incompatible with the inherent dignity of the human person. Therefore we recommend the following:

▶ The World Conference should urge the development and adoption of stronger measures against sexual exploitation and trafficking in women as a violation of human rights. States should be obliged to adopt laws and policies addressing local and global situations including conditions that render women vulnerable to sexual exploitation. States should also be required to prosecute perpetrators and provide for restitution, services and assistance to victims.

6. In consideration of the relationship between Development, Democracy, and Human Rights, it should be recognized that neo-liberal policies and structural adjustment programmes, as well as continuing manifestations of colonialism, negate economic, social and cultural rights, and civil and political rights. The impact that these policies have on women, manifesting itself in the "feminization of poverty," is one of the many ways of further extending the discrimination against, and subordination of women. Development is, and remains, a cultural, social and economic process which is essential for the respect of human rights. Structural adjustment policies should be examined in relation to discrimination against women because they are obstacles to women's enjoyment of the Right to Development.

Another obstacle to the right to development and the full enjoyment of human rights, especially those of women and children, is the violation of the right to self-determination, and the interference of one state in the internal affairs of another. Interference may take different forms, including economic pressure and the imposition of economic blockades which affect access to food, medicine, and other essential commodities and services. This amounts to cruel and inhuman treatment of an entire population, often resulting in violations of the right to life.

We urge this Conference to recognize that true democracy, human rights and peace are incompatible with poverty and exploitation, of which women and children are the greatest victims, and to affirm and propose initiatives and mechanisms to implement the indivisibility of political, civil, social, economic, and cultural rights and the right to development. Where social and economic rights are denied and the state abdicates responsibility for assuring life and well-being (food, shelter, work, health, access to land and other economic resources, welfare, and education) women bear disproportionately the burden of sustaining life and livelihood in human settlements and in sustaining the environment. Therefore we call upon the Conference to consider:

▶ Measures to bring about an end to policies of structural adjustment, and anti-labor decrees and legislation which lead to violations of economic, social and cultural rights. Such policies have a particularly severe and discriminatory impact on women. In the name of structural adjustment, the social, economic and political rights which women have obtained should not be weakened or rescinded.

▶ Review of the international financial institutions and arrangements with a view to establishing a more just economic order that guarantees the economic rights of women and to achieving sustainable development in all countries. Women from all sectors, including peasant women, should be involved in the development process, and have effective participation in the decision-making at all levels. International institutions regulating trade, finance and aid should not create conditions that lead to violations of economic, social and cultural rights and should be accountable to United Nations human rights bodies.

▶ Procedures to implement social and economic rights, including an optional protocol providing for individual and group complaints under the International Covenant on Economic, Social and Cultural Rights (ICESCR), and to ensure the accountability of States to undertake affirmative measures to guarantee these rights.

▶ Measures which would bring an end to economic blockades which affect the free flow of food, medicines, and other essential commodities and services due to their inhuman and life-threatening character.

7. In considering the full realization of women's human rights, attention must be paid to the area of human reproduction. Women have a fundamental right to control their own bodies, their sexuality, and their reproduction, and to accessible and adequate health care and safe motherhood as part of the universal right of all to health care. Women have a right to information, education, and access to family planning and to other reproductive health services, including measures to prevent sexually transmitted diseases and AIDS.

Motherhood must result from a free and informed decision by each woman. Reproductive rights as human rights not only prohibit coercion or abuse as a result of State laws, population policies and social customs, but also entitle women to affirmative efforts on the part of States and international organizations to foster the social, economic and cultural conditions that will ensure their inviolability, self-determination, health, and livelihoods consistent with respect for the diversity among women. Such conditions include access to a wide choice of safe contraceptives for women and men, back-up alternatives, safe abortion, and maternity services provided through participatory, consensual processes, as recognized in the Convention on the Elimination of All Forms of Discrimination Against Women.

These rights are particularly important for women during childhood and adolescence, when their right to life, health, and their development is threatened due to exploitation, discrimination, abuse, forced pregnancy and lack of educational opportunities. Therefore we recommend the following:

◗ The World Conference should encourage governments to protect the right of women to the enjoyment of the highest attainable standard of physical and mental health affirmed in the International Covenant on Economic, Social and Cultural Rights, the Convention on the Elimination of All Forms of Discrimination Against Women and the 1968 Teheran Declaration.

◗ Ensure that women's right to accessible and quality health care includes their right to the widest possible choice of family planning and other reproductive health services and education to maximize their health and well-being during all stages of their life span.

◗ Urge governments to protect women's right to liberty and security affirmed in the International Covenant on Civil and Political Rights by ensuring their free and informed consent to reproductive and health services and by preventing any kind of discrimination, abuse or coercion.

◗ Encourage governments to work towards eliminating social practices regarding sexuality and early marriage that are harmful to health and result in the denial of a girl's right to growth and development.

8. In their Declaration for the Bangkok Regional Conference, the Asian NGOs stated: "We can learn from different cultures in a pluralistic perspective and draw lessons from the humanity of these cultures to deepen respect for human rights....Universal human rights standards are rooted in many cultures. We affirm the basis of universality of human rights which afford protection to all of humanity, including special groups such as women, children, minorities and indigenous peoples, workers, refugees and displaced persons, the disabled [persons with disabilities] and the elderly. While advocating cultural pluralism, those cultural practices which derogate from universally accepted human rights, including women's rights, must not be tolerated. As human rights are of universal concern and are universal in value, the advocacy of human rights cannot be considered to be an encroachment upon national sovereignty."

Regarding the universality of human rights, all international instruments should be applied equally to all women and governments should not use cultural and religious issues as a shield to evade responsibility for defending the fundamental human rights of women. We also note with concern the systematic violations of women's rights in states where governments are based on religious fundamentalism. In consideration of the need to ensure the universality of human rights, we recommend the following:

▶ Governments should devise measures to counter all forms of religious intolerance or cultural practices which deny women's human rights and liberties, including those forms of religious intolerance and cultural practices which deny the human rights and liberties of lesbian women.

▶ The Commission on Human Rights should appoint a Special Rapporteur responsible for monitoring and reporting on the situation of women in states where governments are based on religious fundamentalism.

9. Regarding Contemporary Trends in the challenges to the full realization of all human rights of women and men, the World Conference should endorse policy and operational guidelines to ensure full integration of human rights components into United Nations peace-keeping operations, emergency response mechanisms, election monitoring activities and humanitarian assistance initiatives. These guidelines should be aimed at integrating human rights considerations in the planning, implementation, and follow-up to all such activities. In particular, such guidelines must include effective procedures to prevent violations of women's human rights in situations of international and internal armed conflict or ethnic conflict, and effective humanitarian assistance and other measures for protection of women in such situations. The United Nations should assure the protection of women and children by establishing effective monitoring and reporting procedures in areas under the de facto control of its peace-keeping and peace-making missions.

Systematic crimes against women are crimes against humanity, and the failure of governments to prosecute those responsible implies complicity. In order to ensure that those responsible for abuses against women in such situations will be brought to justice, we recommend that:

▶ A permanent international criminal court should be established with universal jurisdiction over war crimes and crimes against humanity, as well as gross and systematic violations of fundamental human rights, including specific abuses of women, such as rape, sexual slavery, forced sterilization, and forced pregnancy. Such a court should have jurisdiction over crimes committed by United Nations personnel as well as by State officials and individuals.

10. With respect to women political prisoners and women living in exile, the World Conference should give consideration to measures which will protect them from gender-specific abuses such as rape and sexual harassment, as well as to measures which will address their gender-specific needs, both in seeking their liberation and when addressing the particular situation of mothers and women needing special (medical, nutritional, etc.) treatment.

11. With respect to refugee women, the Conference should consider their gender-specific needs both in seeking refugee status as well as in the particular situations they face as refugees. Also, the many internal armed conflicts around the world continue to produce women and children who are displaced within their own countries. Such women and girl children face systematic violations of their human rights, including abductions, rapes, and lack of access to food and means of livelihood. We urge the World Conference to consider the following:

▶ Call for international and national measures recognizing feared or actual persecution based on gender, including persecution of women based on religious fundamentalism, as a basis for refugee status and political asylum. Such measures should include modification of the definition of refugee under the 1951 Convention Relating to the Status of Refugees and the 1967 Protocol to this Convention.

▶ Governments should be urged to implement immediately the 1991 Guidelines on the Protection of Refugee Women issued by the United Nations High Commissioner for Refugees. In conformity with the 1991 Guidelines, gender-based persecution must encompass rape and domestic violence and other forms of privately inflicted gender-specific violence where it occurs with the "consent or acquiescence" of the state or "where a government cannot or will not protect women...[even though] the government need not itself have been the instigator of the abuse." The recently adopted (1993) Canadian "Guidelines on Women Refugee Claimants Fearing Gender-Related Persecution" provide a thoughtful guide on gender-based refugee status.

▶ Recognizing that women and children comprise the vast majority of the world's refugees and internally displaced persons, their right to citizenship, health, safety, work and education must be recognized and ensured. This includes protection from physical and sexual abuse in general and from such abuse when it is imposed as a condition for receiving aid and basic necessities. Women refugees and those who are internally displaced have a right to access to medical and health care, including means to prevent or interrupt pregnancies, pre-natal, maternity, and post-natal care. They must be assured access to education, language instruction, employment opportunities, and participation in governance and community development programs on an equal basis with men and boys.

▶ The United Nations and its agencies should extend their peace-keeping activities to areas where there is internal armed conflict. As part of their peace-keeping activities, United Nations personnel should monitor and report on violations which affect women and children.

▶ Humanitarian agencies should consider the plight of internally displaced persons and pay attention to the special needs of women and children in such situations. They should also provide more women staff members to work with displaced women and children.

12. With respect to migrant workers, the World Conference should give consideration to gender-specific abuses, including the trafficking of women, forced prostitution and sexual abuse. Further, it should address migrant women's needs for access to medical care and basic social services, legal resources, the possibility of family reunification, and education for their children. Migrant women should be given an independent legal (residental) status and real opportunities to attain economic independence. We urge the World Conference to consider the following:

▶ Call upon governments to ratify and implement the International Convention on the Protection of the Rights of All Migrant Workers and Members of Their Families.

▶ Call upon governments to adopt legislation and other measures necessary to protect migrant workers from discrimination, abuse and exploitation.

13. The World Conference should consider the full participation of women in politics as indispensable to overcome male domination in public office and all institutions of democracy. We urge the World Conference to declare that women's access to decision-making power in all fields should be a worldwide priority and recommend the following:

▶ Call upon national governments to set goals and timetables to secure equal representation of women at all levels of decision-making, including in decision-making bodies in politics, development and the economy, and to establish measures for the effective implementation of them.

14. The United Nations should set goals and timetables to secure equal representation of women from diverse backgrounds on all United Nations treaty committees and among the special rapporteurs and working groups established by the Commission on Human Rights, the Sub-Commission on Prevention of Discrimination and Protection of Minorities and under the Programme on Advisory Services in Human Rights. Other important measures that could be taken by the United Nations include:

▶ Strengthen the implementation of human rights and the interdependence and indivisibility of economic, social, cultural, civil and political rights by ensuring that gender-specific information drawn from a variety of women's experiences and gender analysis be included in consideration of all human rights, and of the means for advancing the equal realization of all human rights.

▶ Recognize the accountability of United Nations delegates, personnel and other agents of the United Nations, for human rights violations, including gender-specific abuses, and develop procedures for implementing this accountability.

▶ Simplify the prerequisites of the United Nations bodies for the exhaustion of national remedies so that the time, cost, and inconvenience of pursuing internal remedies no longer presents an obstacle to the effective enforcement of human rights.

15. To ensure the effective contribution to the advancement of human rights by the specialized agencies of the United Nations (such as UNESCO, ILO and WHO, as well as other branches of the United Nations, such as UNDP) whose work bears upon the implementation of women's human rights, we recommend that the following steps should be taken:

▶ Consider measures to integrate gender-specific information and analysis in the work of specialized agencies, including training for relevant personnel and the participation of women affected in the development and evaluation of programmes and initiatives.

▶ Develop effective mechanisms for dialogue and information exchange between the specialized bodies and the international and regional human rights bodies.

▶ Develop mechanisms for overview and periodic evaluation of the effectiveness of these procedures.

▶ Prepare a report on the effectiveness of these initiatives for the 1995 World Conference on Women in cooperation with NGOs active in the field.

▶ Ensure the provision of adequate financial and human resources for these purposes.

16. **Human rights education is a fundamental human right. The World Conference should reaffirm that United Nations bodies and governments have an obligation to disseminate human rights information, to support national and grassroots NGOs working to create human rights awareness, and to help communities protect themselves against violations. Human rights information and materials including those which guarantee and explain women's rights should be translated into national languages and widely disseminated.**

Furthermore, the promotion of women's human rights requires that all United Nations publications relating to human rights teaching, peace and international education contain information about existing instruments which address women's human rights, in particular, CEDAW.

17. **United Nations bodies should develop procedures to expand the access of NGOs with expertise regarding women's human rights to all United Nations structures and activities relating to human rights, including the work of the specialized agencies and other bodies.**

18. **The World Conference should call upon regional human rights bodies to implement the foregoing recommendations in their respective contexts so as to further the enforcement of international human rights, including women's human rights.**

Document F
Excerpts from The Vienna Declaration and Programme of Action

The following excerpts from the Vienna Declaration, specifically address the rights of women and girls:

Excerpt from Section I.

18. The human rights of women and of the girl-child are an inalienable, integral and indivisible part of universal human rights. The full and equal participation of women in political, civil, economic, social and cultural life, at the national, regional and international levels, and the eradication of all forms of discrimination on grounds of sex are priority objectives of the international community.

Gender based violence and all forms of sexual harassment and exploitation, including those resulting from cultural prejudice and international trafficking, are incompatible with the dignity and worth of the human person, and must be eliminated. This can be achieved by legal measures and through national action and international cooperation in such fields as economic and social development, education, safe maternity and health care, and social support.

The human rights of women should form an integral part of the United Nations human rights activities, including the promotion of all human rights instruments relating to women.

The World Conference on Human Rights urges Governments, institutions, intergovernmental and non-governmental organizations to intensify their efforts for the protection and promotion of human rights of women and girl-child.

28. The World Conference on Human Rights expresses its dismay at massive violations of human rights especially in the form of genocide, "ethnic cleansing" and systematic rape of women in war situations, creating mass exodus of refugees and displaced persons. While strongly condemning such abhorrent practices it reiterates the call that perpetrators of such crimes be punished and such practices immediately stopped.

29. The World Conference on Human Rights expresses grave concern about continuing human rights violations in all parts of the world in disregard of standards as contained in international human rights instruments and international humanitarian law and about the lack of sufficient and effective remedies for the victims.

The World Conference on Human Rights is deeply concerned about violations of human rights during armed conflicts, affecting the civilian population, especially women, children, the elderly and the disabled. The Conference therefore calls upon States and all parties to armed conflicts strictly to observe international humanitarian law, as set forth in the Geneva Conventions of 1949 and other rules and principles of international law, as well as minimum standards for protection of human rights, as laid down in international conventions.

The World Conference on Human Rights reaffirms the right of the victims to be assisted by humanitarian organizations, as set forth in Geneva Conventions of 1949 and other relevant instruments of international humanitarian law, and calls for the safe and timely access for such assistance.

30. The World Conference on Human Rights also expresses its dismay and condemnation that gross and systematic violations and situations that constitute serious obstacles to the full enjoyment of all human rights continue to occur in different parts of the world. Such violations and obstacles include, as well as torture and cruel, inhuman and degrading treatment or punishment, summary and arbitrary executions, disappearances, arbitrary detention, all forms of racism, racial discrimination and apartheid, foreign occupation and alien domination, xenophobia, poverty, hunger and other denials of economic, social and cultural rights, religious intolerance, terrorism, discrimination against women and lack of rule of law.

Excerpt from Section II.
B. Equality, Dignity and Tolerance

36. The World Conference on Human Rights urges the full and equal enjoyment by women of all human rights and that this be a priority for Governments and for the United Nations. The World Conference on Human Rights also underlines the importance of the integration and full participation of women as both agents and beneficiaries in the development process, and reiterates the objectives established on global action for women towards sustainable and equitable development set forth in the Rio Declaration on Environment and Development and chapter 24 of Agenda 21, adopted by the United Nations Conference on Environment and Development (Rio de Janeiro, Brazil, 3-14 June 1992).

37. The equal status of women and the human rights of women should be integrated into the mainstream of United Nations system-wide activity. These issues should be regularly and systematically addressed throughout relevant United Nations bodies and mechanisms. In particular, steps should be taken to increase cooperation and promote further integration of objectives and goals between the Commission on the Status of Women, Commission on Human Rights, the Committee for Elimination of Discrimination against Women, the United Nations Development Programme and other United Nations agencies. In this context, cooperation and coordination should be strengthened between the Centre for Human Rights and the Division for the Advancement of Women.

38. In particular, the World Conference on Human Rights stresses the importance of working towards the elimination of violence against women in public and private life, the elimination of all forms of sexual harassment, exploitation and trafficking in women, the elimination of gender bias in the administration of justice and eradication of any conflicts which may arise between the rights of women and the harmful effects of certain traditional or customary practices, cultural prejudices and religious extremism. The World Conference on Human Rights calls upon the General Assembly to adopt the draft declaration on violence against women in accordance with its provisions. Violations of the human rights of women in situations of armed conflict are violations of the fundamental principles of international human rights and humanitarian law. All violations of this kind, including in particular murder, systematic rape, sexual slavery, and forced pregnancy, require a particularly effective response.

39. The World Conference on Human Rights urges the eradication of all forms of discrimination against women, both hidden and overt. The United Nations should encourage the goal of universal ratification by all States of the Convention on the Elimination of All Forms of Discrimination against Women by the year 2000. Ways and means of addressing the particularly large number of reservations to the Con-

vention should be encouraged. Inter alia, the Committee on the Elimination of All Form of Discrimination against Women should continue its review of reservations to the Convention. States are urged to withdraw reservations that are contrary to the object and purpose of the Convention or which are otherwise incompatible with international treaty law.

40. Treaty monitoring bodies should disseminate necessary information to enable women to make more effective use of existing implementation procedures in their pursuits of full and equal enjoyment of human rights and non-discrimination. New procedures should also be adopted to strengthen implementation of the commitment to women's equality and human rights of women. The Commission on the Status of Women and the Committee on the Elimination of Discrimination against Women should quickly examine the possibility of introducing the right of petition through the preparation of an optional protocol to the Convention on the Elimination of All Forms of Discrimination against Women. The World Conference on Human Rights welcomes the decision of the Commission on Human Rights to consider the appointment of a special rapporteur on violence against women at its fiftieth session.

41. The World Conference on Human Rights recognizes the importance of the enjoyment by women of the highest standard of physical and mental health throughout their life-span. In the context of the World Conference on Women and the Convention on the Elimination of All Forms of Discrimination against Women, as well as the Proclamation of Teheran of 1968, the World Conference on Human Rights reaffirms, on the basis of equality between women and men, a woman's right to accessible and adequate health care and the widest range of family planning services, as well as equal access to education at all levels.

42. Treaty monitoring bodies should include the status of women and the human rights of women in their deliberations and findings, making use of gender-specific data. States should be encouraged to supply information on the situation of women de jure and de facto in their reports to treaty monitoring bodies. The World Conference on Human Rights notes with satisfaction that the Commission on Human Rights adopted at its forty-ninth session resolution 1993/46 of 8 March 1993 stating that rapporteurs and working groups in the field of human rights should also be encouraged to do so. Steps should also be taken by the Division for the Advancement of Women in cooperation with other United Nations bodies,

specifically the Centre for Human Rights, to ensure that the human rights activities of the United Nations regularly address violations of women's rights, including gender-specific abuses. Training for United Nations human rights and humanitarian relief personnel to assist them to recognize and deal with human rights abuses particular to women and to carry out their work without gender bias should be encouraged.

43. The World Conference on Human Rights urges Governments and regional and international organizations to facilitate the access of women to decision-making posts and their greater participation in the decision-making process. It encourages further steps within the United Nations Secretariat to appoint and promote women staff members in accordance with the Charter of the United Nations, and encourages other principal and subsidiary organs of the United Nations to guarantee the participation of women under conditions of equality.

44. The World Conference on Human Rights welcomes the World Conference on Women to be held in Beijing in 1995 and urges that human rights of women should play an important role in its deliberations, in accordance with the priority of the World Conference on Women of equality, development and peace.

Document G
Principal UN Bodies Concerned with Human Rights Promotion and Protection

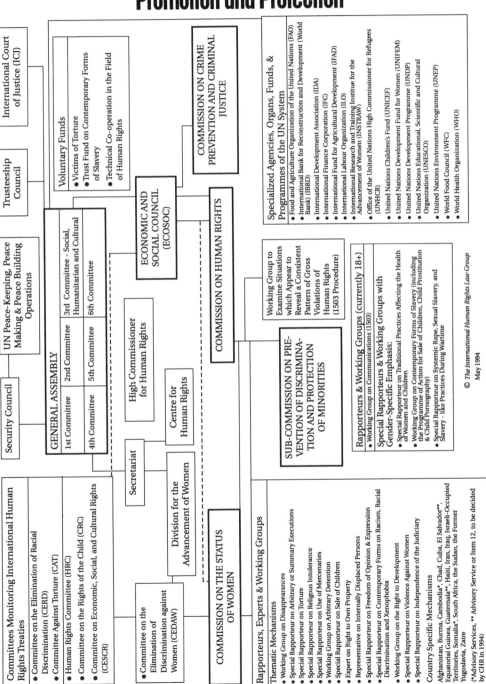

© The International Human Rights Law Group
May 1994

Document H
Global Campaign Resources and Contacts

Note: These are resources primarily related to the Global Campaign and the World Conference on Human Rights in Vienna, June 1993. For a more complete bibliography on the human rights of women, see Women and Human Rights *by Katarina Tomaševski listed below.*

Akina Mama wa Afrika. Special Issue: *African Women and Human Rights. African Woman.* No. 8, December 1993-May 1994. Contact: Akina Mama wa Afrika, London Women's Centre, 4 Wild Court, London, England, WC2B 4AU; fax (44-71) 831-3947.

Aldé, Alessandra, ed. *Terra Femina: Women and Human Rights.* Institute of Cultural Action (IDAC): Rio de Janeiro, Brazil 1993. Contact: IDAC-Institute of Cultural Action, Lopes Quintas 211—Jardim Botânico, 22460-010 Rio de Janeiro, R.J. Brazil.

Amnesty International. *Women in the Front Line: Human Rights Violations Against Women.* Amnesty International Publications: New York, USA, 1991. Contact: Amnesty International Publications, 322 Eighth Avenue, New York, NY 10001 USA.

Amnesty International USA. *Breaking The Silence: Human Rights Violations Based on Sexual Orientation.* Amnesty International Publications: New York, USA, 1994. Contact: see above.

Ashworth, Georgina. *Changing the Discourse: A Guide to Women and Human Rights.* CHANGE: London, England, 1993. Contact: CHANGE, P.O. Box 824, London SE 9JX, England; fax (44-71) 277-6187.

ASMITA, Resource Centre for Women. *Workshop on Gender Violence and Human Rights,* Secunderabad, India, December 1992. Contact: ASMITA, Resource Centre for Women 4-3-12, R.P. Road, Secunderabad 500 003, A.P., India.

Broadbent, Edward. "What Should the World Conference Accomplish?" *Libertas: ICHRDD Newsletter.* International Centre for Human Rights and Democratic

Development (ICHRDD). Vol. 3, No. 3, June 1993. Contact: ICHRDD, 63 Rue de Bresole, Montreal, Québec, H24 1V7, Canada; fax (1-514) 283-3792.

Butegwa, Florence. *The World Conference on Human Rights: The WiLDAF Experience.* Women in Law and Development in Africa: Harare, Zimbabwe, 1993. Contact: WILDAF, P.O. Box 4622, Harare, Zimbabwe; fax (263-4) 731901/2.

Bunch, Charlotte. "Women's Rights as Human Rights: an international lobbying success story." *Human Rights Tribune Special Issue: UN World Conference on Human Rights.* Vol. 2, No. 1, June 1993. Contact: Human Rights Internet, University of Ottawa, 57 Louis Pasteur, Ottawa, Ontario, K1N 6N5, Canada; fax (1-613) 564-4054.

Bunch, Charlotte. "How it was Done: The Movement that Put Women's Human Rights on the Global Agenda." *The International Communication Project News Letter.* No. 15, June/July 1993. Contact: NEWSLETTER c/o AStA Universität Hannover, Welfengarten 1, 30167 Hannover, Germany.

Byrnes, Andrew. "Towards More Effective Enforcement of Women's Human Rights Through the Use of International Human Rights Law and Procedures." Prepared for the *Consultation on Women's International Human Rights,* Faculty of Law, University of Toronto, Toronto, Canada, 1992. Contact: Andrew Byrnes, Faculty of Law, University of Hong Kong, fax; (852) 559-3543.

Carrillo, Roxanna. *Battered Dreams, Violence Against Women As An Obstacle to Development.* United Nations Development Fund for Women (UNIFEM): New York, USA, 1992. Contact: Women Ink., 777 UN Plaza, 3rd Floor, New York, NY 10017 USA; fax (212) 661-2704.

Carrillo, Roxanna and Melanie Roth. "Women Make Gains at Human Rights Conference." *UNIFEM NEWS.* United Nations Development Fund for Women (UNIFEM). Vol. 1, No. 3, October 1993. Contact: Roxanna Carrillo, UNIFEM, 304 East 45th Street, New York, NY 10017 USA; fax (1-212) 906-6705.

Carrillo, Roxanna and Charlotte Bunch. *Gender Violence: A Human Rights and Development Issue.* Contact: Center for Women's Global Leadership, fax (1-908) 932-1180.

Center for Women's Global Leadership. *Testimonies of the Global Tribunal on*

Violation of Women's Human Rights (1994). Contact: Center for Women's Global Leadership; fax (1-908) 932-1180.

Center for Women's Global Leadership. *Gender Violence and Women's Human Rights in Africa* (1994). Contact: see above.

Center for Women's Global Leadership. *International Campaign for Women's Human Rights Report* 1992-1993. (1993) Contact: see above.

Center for Women's Global Leadership. *Women, Violence and Human Rights: 1991 Women's Leadership Institute Report* (available in English and Spanish). Contact: see above.

Communications Consortium. *The Global Campaign for Women's Human Rights: Making Women's Voices Heard.* Analysis of US news coverage of Women's Human Rights Issues in June 1993. Contact: Joanne Omang, Communications Consortium Media Center, 1333 H Street NW, Suite 700, Washington DC 20005-4707 USA; fax (1-202) 682-2154.

Cook, Rebecca. "State Responsibility for Violations of Women's Human Rights." *Harvard Human Rights Journal.* Vol. 7, 1994.

Cook, Rebecca. "Accountability in International Law for Violations of Women's Rights by Non-State Actors." Delivered at the *American Society of International Law* annual meeting, 1993. Contact: Rebecca Cook, International Human Rights Programme, 78 Queen's Park, University of Toronto Law School, Toronto M5S 2C5 Canada, fax; (1-416) 978-7899.

Dieng, Adama, ed.. *The UN Conference on Human Rights,* Vienna, June 1993. Special issue of the International Commission of Jurists Review. No. 50, 1993. Contact: International Commission of Jurists (IJC), P.O. Box 160, CH-1216 Geneva, Switzerland, or AAIJC, 777 UN Plaza, New York, NY 10017 USA.

FIRE (Feminist International Radio Endeavor—at RFPI), ILANUD (United Nations Latin American Institute for Crime Prevention and the Treatment of Offenders), and Emma Hilario of Comedores Populares in Peru. *Report on Post-Vienna Activities in Costa Rica,* 1993. Contact: FIRE at RFPI, Apartado 88, Santa Ana, Costa Rica; fax (506) 249-1929/249-1095, or ILANUD, Apartado 10071-10000, San José, Costa Rica; fax (506)233-7175/253-4912.

Freedom House. *Human Rights: Showdown in Vienna.* Freedom Review Special Issue. Vol. 24, No. 5, October 1993. Contact: Freedom Review, 120 Wall Street, New York, NY 10005 USA.

Freeman, Marsha. *Human Rights in the Family: Issues and Recommendations for Implementation.* International Women's Human Rights Action Watch (IWRAW). April 1993. Contact: IWRAW/WPPD, Humphrey Institute, 301 19th Avenue South, Minneapolis, Minnesota 55455 USA; fax (1-612) 625-6351.

Gessen, Masha. *The Rights of Lesbians and Gay Men in the Russian Federation: An International Gay and Lesbian Human Rights Commission Report.* IGLHRC: San Francisco, California, USA, 1994. Contact: IGLHRC, 514 Castro Street, San Francisco, CA 94114 USA; fax (1-415) 255-8662.

Hewitt, Elaine. "Human Rights and Women." *CAFRA News*. Caribbean Association for Feminist Action and Research (CAFRA). Vol. 7, No. 2, June 1993. Contact: CAFRA News, P.O. Box 442, Tunapuna Post Office, Trinidad and Tobago, West Indies; fax (809) 663-6482.

Human Rights Watch. *Human Rights Watch World Report 1994.* Human Rights Watch Publications: New York, NY, 1994. Contact: Human Rights Watch, Publications Department, 485 Fifth Avenue, New York, NY 10017-6104 USA.

Human Rights Watch. *Indivisible Human Rights.* Human Rights Watch Publications: New York, NY, 1992.

Human Rights Watch Women's Project. *Rape in Haiti: A Weapon of Terror. A Matter of Power: State Control of Women's Virginity* (Turkey), 1994. *Thailand: Trafficking of Burmese Women & Girls,* 1993. *Widespread Rape of Somali Women Refugees in NE Kenya,* 1993. *Rape in Kashmir: A Crime of War* (India), 1993. *War Crimes in Bosnia-Herzegovina: Volume II.,* 1993. Human Rights Watch Publications: New York, NY, 1994. Contact: See above.

Goldberg, Suzanne B.. "Give Me Liberty or Give Me Death: Political Asylum and the Global Persecution of Lesbians and Gay Men." *Cornell International Law Journal.* Vol. 26, No. 3, 1993.

Informal Sector Service Centre (INSEC). "Nepalese Women and Human Rights" (Appendix 6.4) in *Human Rights Year Book 1993.* INSEC: Kathmandu, Nepal, 1993.

Contact: INSEC, P.O. Box 2726, Kathmandu, Nepal; fax (977-1) 226820 (attn: INSEC).

Informal Sector Service Centre (INSEC). *Women's Initiation to Fight Against Victimization of Women: A Report of the Victim Women's Forum*, Nepalgunj, February 1993. Contact: see above.

International Centre for Human Rights and Democratic Development (ICHRDD). "Precarious Progress in Vienna." *Libertas: ICHRDD Newsletter*. Vol. 3, No. 4, September 1993. Contact: ICHRDD, 63 Rue de Bresoles, Montreal, Québec, H24 1V7, Canada; fax (1-514) 283-3792.

International Centre for Human Rights and Democratic Development (ICHRDD). "Making Women's Rights Part of the Global Human Rights Agenda." *Libertas: ICHRDD Newsletter*. Vol. 2, No. 3, June 1992.

International Human Rights Law Group. *Token Gestures: Women's Human Rights and UN Reporting: The UN Special Rapporteur on Torture*. June 1993. Contact: Women in the Law Project, International Human Rights Law Group, 1601 Connecticut Avenue NW, Suite 700, Washington DC 20009 USA.

International Union of Students (IUS). *IUS Women's Newsletter Special Issue*. IUS: Prague, Czech Republic. No. 2, August 1993. Contact: Editor, IUS Women's Newsletter, 17th November Street, P.O. Box 58, CS-110 01 Prague 1, Czech Republic; fax (42-2) 231-6100.

International Women's Tribune Centre. *The Tribune: A Women and Development Quarterly*. Especially No. 46 *Violence Against Women* (June 1991); *A Call to Action* (March 1993); *Women's Human Rights: Vienna 1993* (June 1993), and No. 51 *Claiming Our Rights* (March 1994). Contact: International Women's Tribune Centre, 777 UN Plaza, New York, NY 10017 USA; fax (1-212) 661-2704.

ISIS Internacional. *La Mujer Ausente: Derechos Humanos en el Mundo. Ediciones de las Mujeres* No. 15, August 1991. Contact: ISIS Internacional, Casilla 2067, Correo Central, Santiago, Chile.

Kaselitz, Verena and Barbara Kühhas. *Frauenrechte-Menschenrechte: Bestandsaufnahme nach der UN-Weltkonferenz über Menschenrechte* im Juni 1993 in Wien. Arbeitsgruppe Frauenrechte Menschenrechte (Austrian Women's Coalition for

Women's Human Rights), September 1993. Contact: Arbeitsgruppe Frauenrechte Menschenrechte, 1050 Wien, Hofgasse 9/1/4, AUSTRIA.

Kerr, Joanna, ed. *Ours By Right: Women's Rights as Human Rights.* ZED Books and The North South Institute: Ottawa, Canada, 1993. Contact: ZED Books Ltd., 57 Caledonian Road, London, N1 9BU, or ZED Books Ltd., 165 First Avenue, Atlantic Highlands, NJ 07716 USA.

Marin, Leni. "The Global Fight for Women's Rights." *Crossroads.* March 1994. Contact: Institute for Social and Economic Studies, P.O. Box 2809, Oakland, CA. 94609 USA.

Marin, Leni, and Blandina Lansang de Mesa. *Women on the Move: Proceedings of the Workshop on Human Rights Abuses Against Immigrant and Refugee Women* at the World Conference on Human Rights, Vienna, Austria, June 1993. Family Violence Prevention Fund, 1993. Contact: Family Violence Prevention Fund, Building One, Suite 200, 1001 Potrero Avenue, San Francisco, CA 94110, fax; (1-415) 824-3873.

Ortiz Buijuy, Marcela. "Un Tribunal Inedito." *Mujeres en Acción.* ISIS Internacional. No. 3, 1993. Contact: ISIS Internacional, Casilla 2067, Correo Central, Santiago, Chile.

Programa Mujer Y Justicia Penal, ILANUD, con el auspicio de la Embajada de Dinamarca. *Festival Internacional de Arte de Mujeres por Nuestros Derechos Humanos: 25 de Noviembre al 6 de Diciembre, 1992.* San Jose, Costa Rica. Contact: ILANUD, Apartado 10071-10000, San Jose, Costa Rica; fax (506) 233-7175/253-4912.

Rodriguez, Regina. "Protagonismo Femenino en Viena." *Mujeres en Acción.* ISIS Internacional. No. 3, 1993. Contact: ISIS Internacional, Casilla 2067, Correo Central, Santiago, Chile.

Sajor, Lourdes. "Women in Armed Conflict Situations." Prepared for the *Division for the Advancement of Women, DPCSD: Expert Group Meeting on Measures to Eradicate Violence Against Women,* New Jersey, October 1993. Contact: Division for the Advancement of Women/DPCSD, Two UN Plaza, 1216, New York, NY 10017 USA; fax (1-212) 963-3463.

Satellite Meeting *"La Nuestra": Diagnostics and Strategies Concerning Human*

Rights of Women in Latin America and the Caribbean. Report of the "Satellite Meeting" of women's groups and NGO's preceding the Latin American and Caribbean Regional Preparatory Conference to the United Nations World Conference on Human Rights. San José, Costa Rica, December 1992. Contact: María Suárez, FIRE, fax: (506) 249-1821.

Schuler, Margaret. *Claiming Our Place: Working the Human Rights System to Women's Advantage.* Institute for Women, Law and Development: Washington, DC, USA 1993. Contact: IWLD, 733 15th Street NW, Suite 700, Washington DC 20005 USA.

Shallat, Lezak. "Women, Violence and the World Conference on Human Rights." *Women's Health Journal.* Latin American and Caribbean Women's Health Network/ISIS-International. No. 1, 1993. Contact: Latin American and Caribbean Women's Health Network at ISIS Internacional, Casilla 2067, Correo Central, Santiago, Chile; fax (562) 638-31-42.

Sheikh Hashim, Leila, and the Tanzania Media Women's Association. "Striving for Women's Rights within the framework of Human Rights Charters." Presented at the *Human Rights, Democratization and Development* conference organized by NOVIB, The Hague, April 22-25, 1992. Contact: Tanzania Media Women's Association, P.O. Box 6143, Dar es Salaam, Tanzania, fax; 255-51-41905/29347.

Sullivan, Donna. "Women's Human Rights and the 1993 World Conference on Human Rights." *The American Journal of International Law.* Vol. 88, No. 1, January 1994. Contact: Women in the Law Project, International Human Rights Law Group, 1601 Connecticut Avenue NW, Suite 700, Washington DC 20009 USA.

Tomaševski, Katarina. *Women and Human Rights.* ZED Books: New Jersey, USA, 1993. Contact: ZED Books Ltd., 165 First Avenue, Atlantic Highlands, NJ 07716 USA or ZED Books Ltd., 57 Caledonian Road, London N1 9BU, England.

United Nations Centre for Human Rights. *Human Rights: Communications Procedures.* Fact Sheet No. 7. Centre for Human Rights, United Nations Office at Geneva, 1211 Geneva 10, Switzerland.

United Nations Development Fund for Women (UNIFEM). *Putting Women on the Agenda:* Report Submitted by UNIFEM to the World Conference on Human Rights

June 1993. Contact: UNIFEM, 304 East 45th Street, 6th Floor, New York, NY 10017 USA; fax (1-212) 906-6705.

United Nations High Commissioner for Refugees. *Human Rights: the new consensus.* Regency Press: London, UK 1994. Contact: Regency Press (Humanity) Ltd., Gordon House, 6 Lissenden Gardens, London, NW5 1LX, England; fax (44-71) 267-5505.

Voices: Canadian Voice of Women for Peace. Vol. 14, Nos. 1-2, August 1993. Contact: Voice of Women, 736 Bathurst Street, Suite 215, Toronto, Ontario, M5S 2R4, Canada.

Women Living Under Muslim Laws. "Women Living Under Muslim Laws Statement on Women's Human Rights. Prepared for the World Conference on Human Rights, Vienna 1993." *Women Living Under Muslim Laws Newsheet.* Vol. 5, No. 2, 1993. Contact: Women Living Under Muslim Laws, SHIRKAT GAH, 14/300 (27-A) Nisar Road, Lahore Cantt., Pakistan.

Womennews. Women in Development. Vol. 2, No. 3, July-September 1993. Contact: Ministry of Women in Development, Culture and Youth, P.O. Box 7136, Kampala, Uganda.

Women's Action Forum. *Women's Rights as Human Rights: Women's Action Forum Pakistan Position on The Universal Declaration of Human Rights for The World Human Rights Conference,* June 1993. Contact: WAF, 31-F.C.C, Gulberg-IV, Lahore, Pakistan.

Women's Action Network. *Women's Action Network News.* Women's Action Network/Amnesty International. Summer 1993. Contact: see above for Amnesty International Publications.

Women's Infoteka. *Summary: Bread and Roses* (kruh i ruže). Autumn 1993. Contact: Women's Infoteka, Berislavićeva 14, 41000 Zagreb, Croatia; fax (385-41) 422-926.

Women's International Network (WIN). *Women's International Network News,* especially Vol. 19, No. 1-3, 1993. Contact: WIN, 187 Grant Street, Lexington MA 02173 USA.

Conventions, Covenants, Documents, and Declarations:

Organization of American States (OAS). *Inter-American Convention on the Prevention, Punishment and Eradication of Violence Against Women.* CIM/Res. 1 (VI-E/94), 1994. Copies can be obtained from the Commission on Women, OAS, 17th and Constitution Avenue N.W., Washington DC 20006.

United Nations. *Resolution on the Special Rapporteur (Resolution Integrating the Rights of Women into the Human Rights Mechanisms of the United Nations).* E/CN.4/1994/L.8/Rev.1 2 March 1994. United Nations Documents are available at: New York Office, Centre for Human Rights, United Nations, New York, NY 10017 USA or Centre for Human Rights, United Nations Office at Geneva, 1211 Geneva 10, Switzerland.

United Nations. *Declaration on the Elimination of Violence against Women.* A/RES/48/104. 23 February 1994.

United Nations. *World Conference on Human Rights: The Vienna Declaration and Programme of Action.* A/CONF.157/23. 25 June 1993.

United Nations. *The Nairobi Forward-Looking Strategies for the Advancement of Women.* E.85.IV.10/RES40/108. 13 December 1985.

United Nations. *Convention on the Elimination of All Forms of Discrimination Against Women.* RES34/180. 18 December 1979.

United Nations. *International Convenant on Economic, Social and Cultural Rights.* RES2200/A/XXI. 16 December 1966.

United Nations. *International Convenant on Civil and Political Rights.* RES2200/A/XXI. 16 December 1966.

United Nations. *Optional Protocol to the International Covenant on Civil and Political Rights.* RES 2200/A/XXI. 16 December 1966.

United Nations. *Universal Declaration of Human Rights.* RES217/A/III. 10 December 1948.

Video and Audio Programs:

Augusta Productions in collaboration with Center for Women's Global Leadership. *The Vienna Tribunal: Women's Rights are Human Rights (VIDEO)*. Contact: Gerry Rogers, Augusta Productions, 54 Mullock Street, St. Johns, Newfoundland, Canada A1C 2R8; fax (1-709) 579-8090.

FIRE—Feminist International Radio Endeavor. A radio series on the Global Campaign and the Vienna Conference in both English and Spanish; Series in progress of the Global Tribunal in Spanish; *Rompiendo Fronteras*—Video of Tribunal held at the Encuentro for Latin America and the Caribbean in El Salvador, 1993. Contact: María Suárez, FIRE at RFPI, Apartado 88, Santa Ana, Costa Rica; fax (506) 249-1929/249-1095.

National Public Radio. *Global Tribunal* radio programme. Contact: Betty Rogers, National Public Radio, 2025 M Street NW, Washington DC 20036 USA; fax (1-202) 822-2329.

Rosenbluth, Helene. *Women's Rights are Human Rights* radio program for Pacifica Radio and tapes in English of the entire Global Tribunal and selected women's workshops in Vienna. Contact: Helene Rosenbluth, HMR Duplications, 4252 Coolidge Ave., Oakland, CA. 94602, USA.

United Nations Radio and Television Department. Radio Programmes produced for UN Radio. Contact: Diane Bailey, UN Secretariat, Radio and Television Department, Room S-890-U, New York, NY 10017 USA.

Women's Feature Service. *Breaking the Silence: Vienna 1993 (VIDEO)*. Contact: Anita Anand, Women's Feature Service, 49 Golf Links Road, New Delhi, India 110 003; fax (91-11) 4626699; or Rebecca Foster, Women's Feature Service, 20 West 20th Street, Suite 103, New York, NY 10011 USA; fax (1-212) 807-9331.

About the United Nations Development Fund for Women

In 1976, the United Nations General Assembly established the Voluntary Fund for the United Nations Decade for Women, which in 1984, became the United Nations Development Fund for Women (UNIFEM). The Fund was created to provide direct support for women's projects, and to promote the inclusion of women in the decision-making processes of mainstream development programmes. UNIFEM's mission is to support efforts of women in the developing world to achieve their objective for economic and social development and for equality, and by so doing, to improve the qualify of life for women and men alike.

Since 1992, UNIFEM's approach to sustainable human development has increasingly integrated activities that support women's human rights. The response of the Fund's broad-based constituency—women's organizations, donors, partner agencies and the international human rights community—to its human rights activities resulted in the establishment of UNIFEM's Women's Human Rights Programme. The Programme reflects the Fund's commitment to pursuing a long-term strategy that consolidates and strengthens previous initiatives taken to advance the women's human rights agenda.

Additional UNIFEM Publications:

Battered Dreams: Violence Against Women as an Obstacle to Development
by Roxanna Carrillo. (1992). $7.95

An End to Debt: Operational Guidelines for Credit Projects
edited by Ellen Pruyne (1993). $15.95

Another Point of View: A Gender Analysis Training Manual for Grassroots Workers
by A. Rani Parker (1993). $15.95

Focusing on Women: UNIFEM's Experience in Mainstreaming
by Mary Anderson (1993). $7.95

Women and the New Trade Agenda
by Susan Joekes and Anne Weston (1994). $7.95

In the US, add $3.50 for the first book, and .75 for each additional; Outside of the US (surface mail), add $3.25 for the first book, and $1.50 each additional.

To order UNIFEM publications, contact: Women, Ink., 777 United Nations Plaza, Room 3C, New York, NY 10017, USA. Tel: (212) 687-8633; Fax: (212) 661-2704.

About the Center for Women's Global Leadership

The Center for Women's Global Leadership at Douglass College seeks to develop an understanding of the ways in which gender affects the exercise of power and the conduct of public policy internationally. The Center's goals are to build international linkages among women in local leadership that enhance their effectiveness, expand their global consciousness and develop coordinated strategies for action; to promote visibility of women and feminist perspectives in public deliberation and policy-making globally; and to increase participation of women in national and international governing bodies and processes.

The Center's activities are based on seeing women's leadership and transformative visions as crucial in every policy area from democratization and human rights, to global security and economic restructuring. The creation of effective policy alternatives demands the full inclusion of gender perspectives and women in all decision-making processes, and requires an understanding of how gender relates to race, class, ethnicity, sexual orientation and culture.

Center for Women's Global Leadership
27 Clifton Avenue, Douglass College
Rutgers University
New Brunswick, New Jersey 08903 USA
For further information call (1-908) 932-8782; fax (1-908) 932-1180.

Additional Center for Women's Global Leadership Publications:

Testimonies of the Global Tribunal on Violations of Women's Human Rights (1994). $15

Gender Violence and Women's Human Rights in Africa (1994). $7

International Campaign for Women's Human Rights Report 1992-1993. $8

Women, Violence and Human Rights: 1991 Women's Leadership Institute Report (available in English and Spanish). $8

Gender Violence: A Human Rights and Development Issue, by Charlotte Bunch and Roxanna Carrillo (1991). $5

The Vienna Tribunal: Women's Rights are Human Rights, produced by Augusta Productions (September 1994). VIDEO

Prices for the above cover postage and handling by surface mail. For international air mail, add 15% for postage. For orders of 10 or more publications, we offer a 20% discount.

Funders for the Center for Women's Global Leadership, the Global Campaign for Women's Human Rights, and the Vienna Tribunal:

Asia Foundation

CIDA (Canadian International Development Agency)

The Ford Foundation

International Centre for Human Rights and Democratic Development

Joe and Emily Lowe Foundation

John D. and Catherine T. MacArthur Foundation

Netherlands Ministry of Development Cooperation

OXFAM/UK and Ireland

Resourceful Woman's Award

Rockefeller Family Fund

Rutgers, the State University of New Jersey

San Francisco Foundation

Seven Springs Foundation

Shaler Adams Foundation

SIDA (Swedish International Development Authority)

Sister Fund

Tides Foundation

UNIFEM (United Nations Development Fund for Women)

About the Authors

Charlotte Bunch, a feminist writer and organizer for over two decades, was a founder of *Washington D.C. Women's Liberation* and of *Quest: A Feminist Quarterly*. She has edited seven anthologies including a collection of her essays, *Passionate Politics: Feminist Theory in Action*. Bunch is a Professor in the Bloustein School of Planning and Public Policy at Rutgers University and is the founding Director of the Center for Women's Global Leadership.

Niamh Reilly came to the US from Ireland in 1984 and has worked at the Center for Women's Global Leadership for five years. She is responsible for the Center's international campaigns and coordinated *The Vienna Tribunal*. Reilly has an MA in Economics and teaches in the Women's Studies program at Rutgers University. She is currently completing a doctoral thesis in Political Science that examines human rights, gender and political transformation since the Universal Declaration for Human Rights.